Willie Reed Grady

JOHN ANDREW-SON.

THE SHIP LAUNCH.

LAWRENCE'S ADVENTURES

AMONG THE

ICE-CUTTERS, GLASS-MAKERS, COAL-MINERS, IRON-MEN, AND SHIP-BUILDERS.

BY

J. T. TROWBRIDGE.

BOSTON:
FIELDS, OSGOOD, & CO.
1871.

UNIVERSITY PRESS: WELCH, BIGELOW, & CO.,
CAMBRIDGE.

PREFACE.

THESE "Adventures" of Lawrence were written in the faith that instruction could be made entertaining, and that the young might be educated to observe and think while following the by-paths of a story. Contributed originally to "Our Young Folks," their success as magazine papers has led to their republication in this form.

J. T. T.

ARLINGTON, MASS., Dec. 1, 1870.

CONTENTS.

CHAPTER I.

AT THE POND-SIDE.

CHAPTER II.

AMONG THE ICE-CUTTERS.

CHAPTER III.

AMONG THE GLASS-MAKERS.

CHAPTER IV.

AMONG THE COAL-MINERS.

CHAPTER V.

AMONG THE IRON-MEN.

CHAPTER VI.

AMONG THE SHIP-BUILDERS.

LAWRENCE'S ADVENTURES.

CHAPTER I.

AT THE POND-SIDE.

I.

LEARNING TO SWIM.

IT was June when Lawrence came to the pond-side to live. His uncle's house stood on a high green bank; and his aunt gave him an attic room with a window that looked out upon the water. The winding shores were fringed with flags and willows, or overhung by shady groves; and all around were orchards and gardens and meadows.

A happy boy was Lawrence, for he was passionately fond of the water, and he had never lived so near a pond before. The scene from his window was never twice the same. Sometimes the pond was like glass, mirroring the sky and the still trees. Sometimes light breezes swept over it, and sail-boats rode the dancing waves. Then there were the evenings, when clouds of the loveliest colors floated above it, and the moon rose and silvered it; and the mornings, when all the splendors of the new-risen sun were reflected into Lawrence's chamber.

Whenever he had a leisure hour, — for he went to school, and worked in the garden, — he was to be seen rambling by the shore, or rowing away in his uncle's boat; and he found that the faithful performance of his tasks made his sports all the sweeter to him.

As children who play about the water are always in more or less danger of falling into it, Lawrence's uncle had lost no time in teaching him to swim.

"The first thing for you to learn," said the doctor, — for his uncle was a physician, — "is confidence. Plunge your head under water."

Lawrence did so, and came up with dripping hair and face, gasping. The doctor made him repeat the exercise until he neither gasped nor choked.

"That does not hurt you, does it? No. Neither will it hurt you if you sink to the bottom, for you can hold your breath; the water is shallow, and, besides, I am here to help you. Now try to take a single stroke, just as the frogs do. Throw yourself boldly off your feet, and don't be afraid of sinking."

Lawrence, after considerable hesitation, tried the experiment, and found that he could swim a single stroke, and come down upon his feet again without drowning. He tried it again and again, delighted at his success.

"That will do for this lesson," said his uncle. "You have been long enough in the water. Swimming is a fine exercise for boys, and the bath is good for them; but they often make the mistake of staying too long in the water. Especially at first you must be careful: after you get used to it, you can stay in longer. Never go in when you are heated; or if you do, come out again immediately, and continue exercising, so as to keep the pores of your skin open."

Lawrence learned, in his next lesson, to swim two strokes, and in a few days he could swim a rod. His uncle then taught him how to dive.

"You must avoid falling flat on the water; for if you do so, from any great height, it will beat the breath out of your body almost as suddenly as if you struck a board. Learn to keep your eyes open under the water. Some people's nostrils are so large that the water gets into their heads when they dive; if that is the case with yours, it will be well to stuff a little cotton into them."

Lawrence found no trouble of that kind. He was soon able to dive, and pick up pebbles, and to swim beneath the surface. His uncle then taught him how to rescue a drowning person.

"If he is still struggling, you must not let him get hold of you, or he will very likely cause you to drown with him. The safest and readiest method is to pull him up by his hair. Be sure and keep behind him as you bring him to the surface. Do not try to do more than to lift his face out of water, as you swim with him to the shore. The human body is so light that it may be supported in the water by a very slight effort; but it is hard to keep any portion of it much above the surface."

"But what shall I do after I get him to the shore?" asked Lawrence.

"That is something very important to learn, which you will very likely find useful some day, if you live near this pond. Three young people have been drowned in it within five years, two of whom at least might have been saved from death, had the persons with them known how to get them out of the water, or what to do with them after they had got them out."

"I wish you would teach me that," said the boy.

"Very well; I'll give you a practical lesson before long."

II.

HOW THE DROWNED BOY WAS SAVED.

ACCORDINGLY, a few days afterwards, the doctor met Lawrence and his companions as they were coming up from the water, and, seizing his nephew, exclaimed, "You have been drowned, have you?"

"Not to my knowledge," said Lawrence, laughing.

"Yes; you fell from the boat just now, getting water-lilies. You know how to swim, but you got tangled among the weeds, and were three minutes under water. You have just been fished out, and brought to shore. Lie down, sir, for a drowned boy has no business on his feet."

Lawrence, who understood very well what his

uncle meant, dropped down on the grass, and tried to play the part of a drowned person seriously; but he could n't help laughing, and all the while he watched closely to see what was done for him.

"What shall we do, boys?" cried the doctor. "For not a minute is to be lost."

"Carry him home, the first thing," said Tim Hooper.

"No, we have n't time for that, — so many precious minutes would be wasted."

"Put him in a warm bath," said Jake Thomes.

"We could n't do that without carrying him home, or bringing the warm water to him. Besides, the warm bath is hurtful under such circumstances. A person will drown quicker in warm than in cold water. The reason seems to be, that cold water strikes a chill into the blood, so that its circulation is impeded, and less air is required for it in the lungs. The blood goes to the lungs to throw off carbon, and to get oxygen, which is breathed in with the air, of which you know it is a part. When a person drowns, the supply of oxygen is cut off, and the carbonic acid, retained in the blood, poisons it. A person in a swoon may live half an hour under water; for his blood moves so slowly that very little oxygen is required for it, and there is but little carbon to be thrown off. Now if we stimulate the circulation before we manage to get fresh air into the lungs, — as we should if we put him into a warm bath, — you see we should increase the difficulty."

"The first thing I should do would be to go for the doctor," said Lawrence.

"No, you would n't, for you are drowned, and have no voice in the matter. Besides, I am five miles away, attending to a boy who broke his leg falling from a beam in a barn. But fortunately a boy comes up who has been told what to do in such cases, — fortunately indeed, for already too much time has been lost while we were considering what to do, instead of doing it. This boy knows that the first thing necessary is *fresh air in the lungs.* To make sure that the passage to the lungs is open, he turns the patient on his face, in which position any water that may have lodged in his mouth and throat, or anything that may have risen from his stomach and choked him, drops out."

The doctor at the same time turned Lawrence on his face, to illustrate his method.

"In this position, the tongue also falls forward, and opens a passage to the windpipe. But often the tongue is so much swollen that it is necessary to put your finger on the roots of it and press it forward. This should be looked to, and where there is a hand to spare it will be well to keep the tongue in place in that way. Act promptly, and don't be afraid of hurting him. In this case, however, the tongue will take care of itself. All this must be quickly done; and the new-comer hastens to make the patient gasp. He places him on his side, — thus. He rubs his forehead smartly, to bring warmth and sensitiveness to the skin, then dashes cold water upon it. If he has any snuff about him, or hartshorn, or spirits of any kind, he applies them freely to the nostrils. But the drowned boy does not gasp. Then what?"

"Blow in my lungs," said Lawrence.

"But my own breath is exhausted of oxygen, and charged with carbonic acid; and what we want is fresh air. While one of these boys runs for the doctor, and another for dry blankets, this is what the boy who knows does. He loosens your clothes; then turns you down again upon your face, — completely upon your breast, — with one wrist under your forehead, thus, and passes his other hand with a gentle pressure down your back. That compresses the lungs, and drives the bad air out of them. Then, making the other boys help, he turns you again on your side, and partly upon your back, in which position the lungs open again of themselves, and draw in fresh air. Repeat this process six or eight times a minute, — not too often, for the low circulation requires but little air, and too much cools the body. What we want now is to keep the body warm, and to excite circulation. As soon as we have got the artificial breathing started, we strip off all the wet clothes; wrap the body in the blankets which have been brought; let the fresh air blow on the face and chest; rub and slap the body till it is dry and sensitive, and dash cold water upon it; then rub and slap again. If the blankets do not come, throw off your own coats to wrap the body in."

"How long will it take to bring me to?" Lawrence anxiously inquired.

"That depends upon how thoroughly drowned you were. I should not give you up for an hour; but I should not have much hope of you, if I could perceive no movement of the heart, by putting my ear to it, after a quarter of an hour. In five or ten minutes I should expect you to make a little gasp; and after that I should consider you safe.

"Now, boys," the doctor continued, "remember that, as long as nothing is done to put fresh air into the lungs of a drowned person, it is just the same for him as if he remained all that while in the water. So you must be prepared to do all these things with the utmost promptitude."

He then made them take little Tim Hooper and go through with all the movements with him, as he had done with Lawrence, and repeat the process until they were perfect in it.

"If this was taught in every school where children live or play near a pond or river," he said, "more than half the cases of actual death from drowning might be prevented."

The boys laughed, and thought the lesson more a good joke than anything else. They little expected ever to have to practise it. But now see how useful a little knowledge sometimes proves.

December came, and the pond froze over. So thin, however, was the coating of ice that but few boys ventured to go upon it.

"Wait, my boy, a day or two, until the ice is stronger," said the doctor. "Nothing will be lost by waiting; but much will be risked by attempting to skate to-day."

So Lawrence, not without some mutterings of discontent, I am sorry to say, restrained his eagerness to strap on the new skates his uncle had given him, and remained on the shore, watching those who did skate.

Suddenly a boy fell, broke the ice, and went in. Struggling to get out, he slipped under the ice. It was Jake Thomes, one of the boys who had learned the lesson with Lawrence. How little did he imagine, when he laughed at it, that the time would so soon come for it to be practised on him!

"Boy drowned! Boy drowned!" was the cry; and the skaters flew to the rescue.

Lawrence knew that, under such circumstances, his uncle would approve of his going upon the ice, and he started to run to Jake's assistance. But he had scarcely left the shore when he saw the ice give way again, under the weight of two skaters who approached the broken place. There were now three boys in the water.

"This won't do," thought he; and he ran back to the shore. There was a man at work, preparing some hot-beds, in a garden near by. He had already heard the alarm. "Bring planks! a rake!" cried Lawrence.

He seized one of the broad board coverings of the beds, called shutters, and shoved it out before him on the ice. The man followed with another and a long-handled garden-rake. Nothing had yet been done for Jake, who had not been seen since he went down. Other skaters had arrived; but they were engaged in trying to rescue the two boys who had fallen in after him. It was perilous business. The ice was bending and cracking under them, and they could not reach the edge of it without breaking in, like the others. Fortunately, both boys could swim, and they were sustaining themselves by holding on to coats thrown to them over the edge of the ice. Thus far, at every attempt to get out, they had only broken the ice still more.

Lawrence pushed his shutter close up to the broken place, and, lying flat on his breast upon it, looked down into the clear cold water. He could have seen the bottom but for the floating fragments of thin ice, and the ripples formed by the two boys trying to get out.

"Keep still! keep still!" he cried; but that was not easy for two boys in their position to do. As long as the light reflected from the waves danced in his sight, he could see nothing. So he plunged his face into the water, with his eyes open. *Beneath* the surface, they could see very well. And there, lying on the bottom, in about ten feet of water, clinging fast to some weeds, with his red tippet on his neck and his skates on his feet, was Jake Thomes.

He was directly under the ice Lawrence was on. The plunged face came dripping out of the cold water. "The rake!" The man handed it to Lawrence, who thrust it down, hooked one of the teeth into Jake's tippet, and drew him steadily up.

The broad shutter distributed the pressure of his weight over so large a surface of the ice that it did not break, even when he pulled the drenched and lifeless body out.

The situation on the ice being unsafe and awkward, the body was quickly slid ashore on the shutter, and taken to the gardener's house, which was close by the pond. With the other shutter that had been brought, the other two skaters were speedily rescued; and Lawrence had nothing to do but to think of Jake and his uncle's lesson.

"I should n't have stopped to bring him to the house," he said afterwards, "but Peter insisted on it."

Arrived at the house, however, Peter, who was ignorant as an owl of what should be done in the case, left all to the boy.

"O yes! roll him!" said he, "I 've heard that was good, — to get the water out of him."

Lawrence did not stop to explain that the rolling process was not to get the water out, for none could enter the lungs, but to get the air in. He worked vigorously, according to his uncle's directions. Meantime his uncle was sent for; but he was not at home.

Laid out on Peter's kitchen-table, his wet clothes removed, his limbs loosely wrapped in warm blankets, and several persons smartly slapping and rub-

THE DROWNED BOY.

bing them, according to Lawrence's directions, while Lawrence himself, with Peter's assistance, rolled him from his breast to his side, and over again upon his breast, at the same time keeping a finger at the roots of the tongue, — this was the situation in which the drowned boy's mother found him, when, having heard the terrible news, she came running to Peter's house.

But the peril was now nearly over. Jake had gasped slightly once or twice. Then came the agony of recovering consciousness, in the midst of which the doctor arrived.

It was then half an hour from the time when Jake broke through the ice, and it was evident to all, that, if nothing had been done for him all that while, his recovery would have been impossible.

"Well done! well done!" cried the Doctor. "You have made good use of my lesson, boy! Woman, your child is saved."

The hearty praise of his uncle, the joy of the mother, and his own consciousness of having done a good action, made this the happiest day of Lawrence's life.

CHAPTER II.

AMONG THE ICE-CUTTERS.

I.

CUTTING THE ICE.

THE boys — and, I am glad to say, the girls too — had enjoyed a few days of the very finest skating, when one night there came a fall of snow, and the next morning Lawrence, looking from his window, saw the pond covered with a shining white mantle.

"Never mind," said he; "we can sweep places to skate on. A good skater don't care for a space larger than a parlor floor to practise on."

So he went out that afternoon with a shovel and a broom to clear off a little of the snow. He was surprised to find a number of men on the pond before him. They had long chisel-shaped iron bars, with which they were cutting holes in the ice, about five paces apart, all over the pond.

"Look here!" cried Lawrence, running up to one

of them, "what is this for? You 're spoiling our skating."

"Your skating is spoiled already," said the man; and *click! click!* his bar went through the ice again. "Our business would be spoiled too, if we did n't cut these holes."

"I don't see how!"

"I 'll tell you how. This coating of snow prevents the ice from forming. Snow is warm; did you know it? A sheep covered up in a drift will live through a night that would freeze her to death if she was exposed to the weather. Just so, a heavy fall of snow is the best thing in the world to keep strawberries and other plants from winter-killing. It keeps the pond warm in the same way. Ice will form, to be sure, under the snow, but so slow we should n't get half a crop if we did n't cut these holes and let the water through."

"I see," cried Lawrence. "The weight of the snow makes the ice sink a little; that forces the water up, and the water soaks the snow, and then freezes and makes ice."

"Yes, but that top-ice — *snow-ice,* we call it — is good for nothing. It 's only a bother to us, as you will see if you are here when we are cutting. But it don't prevent the ice from forming underneath, as the snow does."

"I understand, — the ice is a good conductor of caloric, and the snow is n't," said Lawrence, who had learned enough of natural philosophy to come to this conclusion. "But why don't you have some sort of horse-scrapers to scrape the snow off?"

"We have horse-scrapers, but now the ice is n't strong enough to bear a horse; that 's the trouble."

"Will it be good skating after the snow soaks and freezes?"

"It will be pretty rough. There 's a good strip along by the Doctor's shore where we don't cut; it is kept for skating and fishing. You can sweep the snow from that, if you like, and cut holes for pickerel too, — a thing that is n't allowed on any other part of the pond."

"How can you prevent it? Do you own the pond?"

"No, but the ice-company have bought the privilege of cutting from all the owners around the pond, and so control it. Pickerel holes would spoil the ice at the time of cutting; besides, the horses would get their legs in them."

Lawrence was very anxious to see the work begin. He skated meanwhile on his uncle's shore, and after the snow-ice had frozen he went all over the pond, — although, as the man had predicted, he found it pretty rough.

Then there came another fall of snow. By this time the ice was firm enough to bear up horses, and the workmen came on it with plank scrapers six feet broad, and scraped the snow all up, like hay, in big windrows stretching across the pond.

Then there came still another snow, accompanied

by sleet, and followed by rain; so that, when the storm was over, the pond was covered with a coarse frozen crust, too hard for the wooden scrapers. This brought out the iron-edged scoop-scrapers, formed for removing either heavy or crusted snow. Each scraper was drawn by a single horse, with a harness which consisted of a simple girth and loops for the shafts.

At last, one bright morning, early in January, Lawrence looked from his window and saw that the ice-harvest had fairly begun. It was Wednesday; there was no school in the afternoon, and as soon as he had eaten his dinner he hastened out to see the ice-cutters.

There were two men fishing on his uncle's shore. Having chopped holes in the ice, they dropped their hooks through them, baited with live minnows which had been caught in the autumn and preserved in tanks for this purpose. Their minnows were in a pail; an axe and three or four pickerel lay on the ice; and each man was watching half a dozen lines sunk in different places, a few yards apart, and adjusted so that a bite at either would pull down a rag of red flannel set up on a stick for a signal.

Lawrence, like most boys, took a lively interest in fishing. But something of still greater interest attracted him to-day; and, stopping but a few minutes to watch the sport, he hastened on to the scene of the ice-cutting.

Two or three hundred men were at work on the pond, in two divisions, one at the upper and the other at the lower end; presenting, with their horses and ice-saws and ice-hooks and cutters and scrapers and planes, a wonderfully animated and busy picture.

He chose to visit the lower end first, because he there expected to find the man whose acquaintance he had already made. He saw some men at work with a long, straight strip of board and a curious-looking instrument, and ran up to them. One got down on his face and took sight across the board at a target, while the others drew the instrument along the edge of it. They thus marked the ice, somewhat as a school-boy draws a straight line with a pencil and ruler.

The man who had taken sight got up, and Lawrence saw that it was his old acquaintance.

"So you 've come to see the ice-cutting. Well, here you have what is properly the beginning of it. We are striking a straight line, which is almost finished."

Three or four more lengths of the board brought them to the target, set up by one of the windrows of snow.

"This board is what we call a straight-edge. Here is an arm to it which we now open; and you see it lies on the ice like a carpenter's square. Now we are to strike another line at right angles with this; and so we lay out our square-cornered fields of any number of acres, which are to be all cut up into such cakes as the ice-man brings you in summer. This instrument we mark with is called a hand-groove.

You see it has seven steel teeth, set one behind another, and riveted in this strong iron back. Each tooth is a quarter of an inch broad, and forms a sharp little plough by itself. The first cuts the slightest groove in the ice; the second is a trifle longer, and cuts a trifle deeper; the third, deeper still; and so on, till the last, which leaves the groove an inch and a half deep."

"You go all around your field in this way?" said Lawrence.

"No, only on two sides. Now see, — here comes an odd-looking horse-machine down the line we have struck. That is what we call a *guide-and-marker*. The *guide* is a smooth-edged blade that runs in the groove we have cut. The *marker* is a cutter made on the same principle with this hand-groove. The two are so fitted and fastened together that, when the guide runs in the groove, the marker cuts another parallel groove twenty-two inches from it."

As the machine approached, Lawrence saw that it was drawn by a single strong rope, fifteen or twenty feet long, which kept it at a distance from the horse. The horse was led by one man, and the machine held by its handles, like a plough, by another. The marker made a crisp, brittle sound, and threw out fine, bright chips, as the teeth cut through the ice; and after it had passed, Lawrence saw that there were two perfectly straight, beautiful grooves instead of one.

Arrived at the corner of the new field, the horse was turned about, and the machine (by means of an

CUTTING THE ICE.

ingenious arrangement) turned over, so that, returning, the guide ran in the freshly cut groove, and another groove was cut by the marker, twenty-two inches farther on.

"In this way," said Lawrence's friend, "the machine goes over the whole field, the last groove it cuts forming the boundary of the other side. Then it commences on this line, which we are here running at right angles with the first, and goes over the whole field the other way, cutting it all up into checkers twenty-two inches square. The marker cuts a groove two inches deep. Now you see another machine following it, drawn by a horse, just the same. But instead of being double, like the guide-and-marker, it is a single instrument, made up of teeth like the marker; only the teeth are longer, and they cut deeper. That we call a four-inch cutter, as it leaves the groove four inches deep. That will be followed by a six-inch cutter, and that by an eight-inch, and that again by a ten-inch. Each cuts two inches, which is about as much as a horse ought to be compelled to do. We have also a twelve-inch cutter, but this ice is not thick enough to require it."

"Do you cut clear through the ice? I should n't think that would do."

"No, indeed. This ice is about fifteen inches thick, and we shall cut it only ten inches. We have harvested ice when it was only ten inches thick, and again when it was twenty-three inches; but that is rare. Sixteen inches is a good average thickness for working."

Lawrence remained with his friend until the second line was struck. By this time a new machine, likewise drawn by a horse, made its appearance. It was the ice-plane, twenty-two inches broad, running between two grooves, and planing off the porous *snow-ice* which has already been described.

"Now," said the man, "we will see how the ice is housed." And he took Lawrence over a field where a hundred men had been at work all the morning.

It was a busy scene. On one side, the six-, eight-, and ten-inch cutters were going. On the other, men were breaking off broad rafts of the grooved ice, and floating them along a canal which had been cut to the ice-houses. Some were cutting through to the water with saws. Others were splitting off the sheets, the ends of which had been thus cut, with iron bars called "barring-off bars." Still others, by means of "calking-bars," were calking with ice-chips the ends of the grooves which were to come in contact with the water.

"The calking," said Lawrence's friend, "is to keep the water from running into the grooves. For if it gets into them, it will circulate all through them, and then freeze, and the ice will be a solid mass again, as if it had n't been grooved at all.

"These rafts, or sheets of cakes, are, you see, thirty cakes long and twelve broad. The ends have to be sawed; but every twelfth groove — in this direction, lengthwise — is cut deeper than the rest, so that one man can easily bar off a sheet. Ice splits very easy from top to bottom, but it is hard to split it in any other direction. Lay a cake up out of water in a warm day, and it will always begin to honeycomb from the top downward. Turning it on its side makes no difference with it; the frost insists on taking down its work first where it began to build it up. This shows that ice has a grain."

II.

HOUSING THE ICE.

THE sheet of three hundred and sixty cakes, being split off, with its grooves all carefully calked around the ends and sides exposed to the water, was then floated off into the canal, and dragged on towards the ice-houses. One man, armed with an ice-hook, — an instrument resembling a pike-pole, — sometimes riding on the sheet, and sometimes walking by the edge of the canal, navigated this checkered raft to the slip, where it was broken up with bars into blocks of six cakes each, by men standing on the platform. Each of these blocks was fastened upon by an iron grapple, and taken by two men and a horse up an inclined plane to the summit of a strong staging built before the windows of a row of white ice-houses. One man guided the horse; the other guided the block along the smooth rails with a wooden handle attached to the grapple. It was lively work, one horse going up after another at a swift pace. At the summit of the staging, the blocks were seized by men with ice-hooks, and shoved along the now slightly declining rails towards the windows where they were wanted. Swiftly sliding, one after another, went the bright crystal masses, to be seized again by men standing at the windows, and whirled into the ice-houses, where, layer upon layer, they were stowed away.

"As soon as the ice in these is built up to the level of this staging, the horses will begin to carry it up the next one" (for there was another staging above the first); "from that we shall fill the houses nearly to the top; then the ice will be completely covered with hay. Each of these vaults," continued Lawrence's friend, as they went up and looked into one of the great, gloomy buildings, into which the blocks went sliding and bouncing, and where several dimly seen men were at work taking care of them, looking like demons in a pit, — "each of these vaults holds five thousand tons of ice. You will see, behind the ice-houses, trains of cars loading at the same time. The cars take the ice to ships in the harbor, and they take it to all parts of the world. We want to cut, this year, sixty-five or seventy thousand tons. Our two hundred and fifty men will cut about five thousand tons a day."

Lawrence noticed that the ice-houses had very thick wooden walls; but his friend said: "Each wall is in reality two walls, two feet apart, with the space between filled in with tan-bark, which is the best thing we have for keeping out the heat."

"Do you ever cut two crops of ice the same season?"

"Seldom. The second freezing makes poor ice compared with the first. I don't pretend to give the reason. There is a great difference in the quality of ice for keeping. Ice cut in melting weather is porous, and won't keep half as long as ice cut in cold weather."

"It seems to me," said Lawrence, as they descended the inclined plane, "machinery might be invented to take the place of these horses in elevating the ice."

"Well, how would you arrange it?"

"I don't know; but I've been thinking you might have two wheels, one at the water down there, and the other at the top of the ice-house; have an endless chain pass over them, hung full of grapples; set it in motion by an ordinary steam-engine; and let the grapples catch the blocks of ice in the slip, and carry them up an inclined plane to the stagings."

The man laughed. "Go to the other end of the pond, and you'll find very much such a machine as you have suggested. A common steam-engine of forty-horse power does the work of a hundred and fifty men and seventy-five horses, and does it quicker and better. We shall elevate all our ice in that way another year."

Lawrence hastened to the upper ice-houses, and saw, to his delight, the operation of the new machine. It was so much like the one he had arranged in his own mind, that he began to consider himself a great inventor. The floating blocks, of two cakes each, were fed into a little slip under the lower wheel, which revolved just over the water. They were there seized by the grapples, which, coming down empty on the upper side of the moving chain, returned loaded on the under side.

Stiff ratan brooms, fastened to the platform, swept the blocks clean, as the grapples carried them up. The crystallized pond-water was thus elevated by this chain-pump, and poured into the ice-house windows, — the rattling and sliding masses, as they flew along the stagings, resembling an endless train of silver-bright cars seen on high bridges in the distance. There were four stagings, one above another, running the whole length of a long row of ice-houses. The ice was elevated at one end, so that one machine answered for all. The blocks were launched by the grapples upon a short inclined plane, which set them sliding down the gently sloping staging to the windows, where they were seized. The houses being filled to the level of one staging, the ice was then, by a slight alteration in the machinery, carried up to the next.

There was something about this harvesting of the ice so brisk and beautiful that Lawrence remained all the afternoon watching it; and more than once, afterwards, he went to spend a delightful hour among the ice-cutters.

CHAPTER III.

AMONG THE GLASS-MAKERS.

I.

THE "GAFFER."

"WELL, Lawrence," said the Doctor, one day, shoving his chair back from the dinner-table, "how do you think of spending this afternoon?"

"I think I shall finish this piece of pie the first thing," said Lawrence. "Then, as I've no lessons to learn, I feel as if I should like to have a good time."

"If you could manage to have what you call a good time, and learn something too, how would that suit you?" Lawrence thought that would suit him better than anything else. "Well," said the Doctor, "I have business down near the Glass Works; you can go with me, if you like, and perhaps we can learn something about making glass."

"Hurrah!" said Lawrence, delighted; and his pie went the way of all pie in the hands of boys of fifteen with more than usual rapidity.

They had just time to walk to the railroad station and step on board the down train as it stopped. It thundered on again, and in half an hour brought them in sight of a building which the boy knew as the Glass Works, and which he had long wished to peep into. His heart beat quick with curiosity; and he began to wonder (for he had never given the subject much thought before) how such an infinite variety of useful and curious articles — window-panes, mirrors, vases, beads, goblets, lamps, lenses of telescopes and microscopes — were fashioned from so brittle a material, and how the material itself was made.

It was a wide-spreading, irregular pile, with brick walls, and two immense, tapering, tall, round chimneys soaring up into the blue sky above its roofs. The train let them off at a platform near by, and then moved on past the rear of the factory.

"Glass works always like to be near a railroad or a wharf, I find," said the Doctor.

Lawrence said he supposed they sent off heavy freights.

"Yes, but those are a trifle compared with the freights that come to them. Look! there is a coal train switching off and backing up to the yard. They buy fuel by the cargo, as we do by the ton, and stuff it up those huge chimneys. But what is so heavy when it goes in is light enough when it goes out." They looked up at the cloud which poured out of one of the great flues, and stretched away horizontally, in a long, black streamer, high over the adjacent city. "Some of it flies off in smoke, which we can see, but more of it in gases, which we cannot see; and the wind might blow away the ashes. Yet," said the Doctor, as they walked on, "not an atom of the coal is really destroyed; it can't be destroyed; it only changes form."

Going around to the front of the factory, they entered a small door beside a large gate, passed through the office, where the Doctor seemed to be acquainted, and thence through rooms full of wonderful things, which Lawrence wished to stop at once and examine. But his uncle said, "No; we shall come around to these in due time. In visiting a place like this, if you really wish to learn much about it, the way is to begin at the beginning. Now let me see."

They entered the spacious rear yard of the factory from one side, just as the coal train backed into it from the other.

"Ah! there is the gaffer!" said the Doctor. "Do you know what a gaffer is?"

"Laugher, one who laughs; quaffer, one who quaffs; gaffer, one who — gaffs, I guess," said Lawrence, smiling; "though what gaffing is, I don't know more than the man in the moon."

"He sees us; we 'll ask him," said the Doctor.

A short, solid-looking man, in an easy slouched hat and a loose business-coat, who was giving a gang of men directions about unloading the coal, left them, on seeing the Doctor, and came and shook hands with him very cordially. Somehow the Doctor seemed to know everybody.

"This is my nephew," — and Lawrence had the

honor of shaking hands with a gaffer. "By the way," added the Doctor, "I have often wondered why it is you are called a gaffer. What is the meaning of the word?"

"I don't know; it's a name we 're called by," said the man. "The foreman of any other factory than glass works is called a foreman or boss, — or superintendent, if you wish to be very smart. But the foreman of a glass-house is always *the gaffer*, — though I doubt if any one can tell you why."

"Ah! I have it! I have it!" cried the Doctor, tapping Lawrence on the shoulder with his cane in such a way that the boy suspected he had "had it" all the while, — for he was a knowing old head, and he had a habit of testing other people's knowledge of a subject before bringing out his own. "But I sha' n't tell; for if it gets out I shall lose the honor of the discovery. I 'll send the word, with the etymology, to one of the big-dictionary makers. For you won't find it in any dictionary as a name applied to the foreman of a glass-house. "You'll find 'GAFFER; AN OLD MAN,' *gaffer* and *gammer* being ancient abbreviations of *grandfather* and *grandmother*."

"I have it! I have it!" cried Lawrence, in his turn, having caught the bait his uncle threw out; for it was also the Doctor's habit, in keeping back his knowledge of a question, to let fall hints which should lead his young friends to solve it for themselves, thus developing their thinking faculties, and fixing more securely in their minds what they learned.

"What, young man! have you got my secret away from me? Prove it."

"*Gaffer* used to mean grandfather, or old man. Now, in some shops, the boss is called old man. Just so, I suppose, he used to be called *gaffer;* and the name has stuck to him, even after its original meaning has been forgotten."

"Very well! capital! But why is it that it is applied only to the glass-house foreman?"

That Lawrence could not explain. But the gaffer himself had an idea on that point, which, coming from one of the name and trade, was certainly entitled to consideration.

"I imagine," he said, "that generally the foremen of glass-houses were older men than the bosses of other trades, for it takes a man who has spent his life in the business, and grown gray in it, to take the management of it. I believe there is no other trade that requires so much care and experience; that must have been especially the case before our modern improvements in building furnaces. Then again, even if other foremen were called gaffers, they might have lost the name, as it went out of use outside of the shop. But while the men of other trades have changed their habits and expressions to suit the times, glass-makers, until within a few years, never changed anything. That was owing to their exclusiveness. They were a class by themselves. Their art was a wonderful one; it was the most ancient of arts, — it was thought perfect, and not to be improved ; they were jealous of its being known to any that were not regularly initiated into it ; and so they kept it shut up from the world, and surrounded by mystery, almost as much as if they had been members of a secret society."

"Well," laughed the Doctor, "three heads are better than one, and I think, together, we have sifted out the meaning of the word *gaffer* pretty thoroughly. And now for getting at the secrets of this mystic order. Gaffer, what have you got to show us? Lawrence, what shall we see first?"

"Let 's see where the coal goes, since we have begun with the coal," said Lawrence.

"Then you 'd like to see the cave," said the gaffer.

II.

A VISIT TO THE CAVE.

LAWRENCE had no more distinct idea of what a glass-house cave was, than he had had of a gaffer. But *cave* sounded romantic. It suggested the subterranean, — something deep and dark and mysterious. So he said, boldly, that he should like very much to see the cave.

"Come with me," said the gaffer. "We use coal for various purposes, but the bulk of it goes the way I 'll show you."

They were going towards one of the great towering chimneys. But, just before reaching it, the gaf-

THE CAVE.

fer, to Lawrence's great delight, turned suddenly and stepped down into a passage that dived (romantically speaking) deep into the earth. The lad and the Doctor followed, leaving daylight and the upper air behind them, and now saw before them a great glow of fire shining in the midst of surrounding darkness. That is to say, in the language of plain fact, they descended a flight of steps into a sort of cellar, from which, I regret to say, daylight was not wholly excluded, and found themselves — But we will let the gaffer speak.

"Here is where we get our draught. We are now under the large chimney, — cone, we call it. It is supported by these piers. Right in the centre, between them, you see that horizontal grate, with the fire from above shining through; that is in the bottom of the furnace, — what we call the eye."

"It's an awful, fiery-red eye!" said Lawrence. "Don't it look like some horrible, one-eyed dragon, shut up there, and glaring down at us through those iron bars?"

"Not at all; not in the least," said the Doctor, who could be dreadfully prosaic when he saw young people inclined to be too romantic. "It looks to me like a very hot fire. I should think your grates would burn out fast."

"They last longer than one would suppose," said the gaffer. "Iron bars like these will stand a couple of years. The draught of cold air rushing up through them, and the dead cinders accumulating, keep them comparatively cool."

"How do you get rid of the clinkers?" said Lawrence, who remembered his bitter experience cleaning the stoves at home. "I suppose you let the fire go out once in a while."

"We let this fire go down about once in five or six years," said the gaffer. "Then it takes three weeks' steady firing up to get a heat we can work with."

"Three weeks!" exclaimed Lawrence, astonished. "Then it would hardly pay to let the fire go down for the clinkers!"

"As for them, we just slip the grate one side, and cut 'em off from the sides of the eye with an instrument we drive up from below. We never let the fire go down till the furnace burns out. The furnace is built inside the cone."

"And where do you melt your glass?"

"In pots set into the furnace, just overhead here, as I will show you by and by. Our glass pots are closed in, so that no impurities from the fire can get into them. That's the way pots have to be arranged, where flint glass is made. But in furnaces where they make common green glass, which they are not so particular about, the pots are left open at the top, for the advantage of getting the direct action of the heat on the melting materials. That lets the flux run over into the fire sometimes, and that spoils the furnace; so that green-glass furnaces have to shut down about once every year."

Just then a being who seemed (to the imagination of the lad, at least, — the Doctor had forgotten his Arabian Nights some years since), — a being who seemed the dark genie of the place, advanced from some dismal recess in which he had lain concealed, and thrust a ponderous iron spear, or lance, through the bars, directly into the eye of Lawrence's dragon, bringing down from it a sudden shower of fiery tears that lighted up the obscurity. In other words, nearer, perhaps, to the literal truth, a strong, curly-headed, grimy fellow came out from one of the coal chambers under the cone, and gave the fire a poke through the grate, — using an extraordinarily long and strong poker, and fetching down, well, I think we may say, without being too fanciful, a meteoric rain of live embers, like the sparks from an exploded rocket.

The being retreated into the darkness; and now Lawrence beheld a wonderful piece of magic, or optical illusion. He noticed that the opening between the piers, beneath the furnace, extended a long way beyond, forming a sort of subterranean gallery, awfully gloomy, to be sure, except that now the very counterpart of his black genie, who had just thrust the iron into the dragon's eye, appeared, and thrust up a similar iron into a similar eye, and brought down a similar shower of flaming tears at the end of the vista. The whole thing looked so much like a reflection, in a wizard's glass, of the scene he had just witnessed, — occurring a few moments behind the usual time when reflections in earthly mirrors take place, — that he would hardly have been surprised to see phantom images of himself, his uncle, and the gaffer suddenly make their appearance at the second genie's elbow.

I am sorry to add that the worthy gaffer immediately dispelled the pleasing illusion by saying, "The cave extends under both cones; there is another opening at the farther end, opposite to this. You see the other fireman poking the other grate."

"Where do you put in the coal?" asked the Doctor.

"I'll show you. Matthew!"

It was rather disappointing to Lawrence to see his swart genie answer to a Christian name, and to observe, as he came near, facing them in the glow of the furnace fire, that he was, after all, only a harmless, good-natured fellow-creature, notwithstanding the coal-dust that blackened him.

"Open the teaze-hole," said the gaffer.

Matthew led the way towards one of the black coal-chambers, and showed a deep, square-shaped orifice, leading up, by an inclined plane, through the thick brick ribs of the cone, into the furnace. It was closed at the farther end by a half-ignited mass of soft coal, which had been packed into it, to stop the draught in that direction.

"This is the teaze-hole, — though how it ever got that name is more than I know," said the gaffer. "Look up in there, and you'll see him open it."

Matthew took a heavy, long-handled iron implement, called a rake, and shoved it clanging up into the passage, removing enough of the soft glowing mass to let the visitors look in and see the dazzling regions of fire beyond, and hear the rushing of air and roaring of flame in the freshly opened vent. Then he tossed a few shovelfuls of coal into the mouth, and shoved them up with his rake through the teaze-hole into the furnace, to show how the thing was done; then the vent was closed again with coal, as before.

"I see you burn bituminous coal here," said the Doctor. "How much a day?"

"This furnace takes about forty tons a week. The other one, which is not quite as large, takes less. The two average upwards of ten tons a day."

Lawrence asked what was the use of so high a chimney.

"That's to make the draught. The higher the chimney, the greater the draught, generally speaking."

"Can you tell why?" the Doctor asked Lawrence.

"I know heated air expands, and so becomes lighter than the same bulk of cold air. Confine it in a chimney, and that makes a suction from below; — as the hot air rises, cold air rushes in to fill its place."

"But why will a tall chimney make a stronger draught than a low one?"

"I suppose," said Lawrence, "the hot air keeps drawing, until it gets out, and is free. It's like a string of horses attached to anything; the longer the string, the more they will pull. But I should think," he added, "that a chimney might be built too high. If the top gets very cold, I should think that would cool the column of air, and deaden the draught; — it would be like having one horse after another drop down at the end of the string."

"That, I believe, is the fact," said the gaffer. "A sheet-iron funnel as high as this cone, exposed to the weather, would make no draught at all to speak of. If you build high, you must build thick, so that the interior of the chimney will hold its warmth all the way up."

"How did people ever manage without chimneys?" said Lawrence; "for I read the other day that they were unknown in ancient times, and that they were considered a luxury, which only the rich could indulge in, even in the age of Queen Elizabeth."

"They made a fire in the middle of the room, wigwam fashion, and let the smoke get out through a hole in the roof the best way it could," said the Doctor.

"Glass-makers must have labored under an inconvenience," said the gaffer. "I have a little book called 'Reminiscences of Glass-Making,' which has drawings in it of the old-fashioned Italian and French glass furnaces. They have no high chimneys; but the smoke is shown coming out of short flues into the room where the blowers are at work. Their draught must have been very uncertain. A fire must have air."

"It is estimated," remarked the Doctor, "that for every pound of bituminous coal near two hundred cubic feet of common air are required to make an economical fire, — that is, to mix with and burn all the gases; and that, in a fire like this, the weight of the air consumed is greater than that of all the other materials that go into the furnace, — coal, ore, everything."

Lawrence looked astonished. "In that case," said he, "when people get in their winter's supply of fuel, and grumble at the cost, they might console themselves by thinking that the biggest part of what they burn they get for nothing; it don't have to come in carts, and they don't have to settle the bill for it."

"And boys of your age don't get the back-ache shovelling it in at the cellar window," said the Doctor. "It comes, as a great many of our blessings do, so bountifully and so invisibly, that we don't appreciate it. It is well to stop and think of such things sometimes."

"Now," said the gaffer, "I'll show you where the melting-pots are made."

III.

THE MELTING-POTS.

EMERGING from the cave, they crossed a corner of the yard, and entered a long brick building, in the first room of which they found a man at work, on a low bench, in the midst of piles of rubbish.

"Here is where the clay of the pots that have been used up in the furnaces is broken up and cleaned. This man, as you see, takes up a piece at a time, and knocks off the glazed side, and the side that has been in contact with the fire. Then it is ready to be pounded up, and used over again."

They passed on to a second room, which was long

and low and gloomy, and contained several bins, in one of which a man appeared, balancing himself on a bar laid across it, like a gymnast.

"It takes the very best quality of clay for melting-pots," said the gaffer. "This comes from Stourbridge, in England. It is first ground in that hopper, and mixed with the burnt clay, then the whole is shovelled into one of these bins, and worked."

They turned to the gymnast, who, Lawrence now saw, was treading a mass of moist clay with his naked feet. Before him was an empty space, extending across the bin, into which he presently got down, and shovelled back, upon the heap he had been treading, more clay from a dense mass at the opposite end. Then he got up, steadying his movements by means of the bar, and began to tread again.

"That don't seem to be very lively work," said Lawrence.

"It 's better than a treadmill," replied the man. "There 's variety about it. For variety I go to shovelling, and then for variety I go to treading."

"But you don't keep at this all the while, — do you?"

"When I begin a batch, I never leave it, except to eat and sleep, till it 's finished. I can't give it any peace."

"How long do you work it?"

"About seven weeks." The man looked up at a chalk-mark on the wall. "I have been five weeks on this."

TREADING THE CLAY.

"Is it possible," said the Doctor, "that clay requires so much manual, or I may say pedal, labor in its preparation?"

"Nothing else will do," said the gaffer. "Machinery has been tried, but there is nothing like the naked foot."

"Could you make as durable pots without putting in the burnt clay?"

"Pots made of raw clay alone would n't stand at all; they would crack. We must put in the old burnt clay to temper them. Now come up stairs."

As the gaffer threw open the door of an upper room, Lawrence fancied that he was taking them to visit a small menagerie. The loft appeared filled with monsters. They resembled exceedingly chubby young elephant calves, as much as anything. But, what was most extraordinary, they were standing about the room, a herd of fifty or more, holding up short round necks, all with their heads cut off! At a second glance he discovered that they were never designed to have heads, or legs either; and that the great hole he found in each pitifully uplifted headless neck was nothing more nor less than the usual opening into the — melting-pot.

These were the finished pots. Others were unfinished. There were two workmen in the room, one of whom was cutting off slices of a thick clay loaf, and making them over into rolls. He cut the slices by means of a wire furnished with a wooden handle at each end; and he shaped the rolls with his hands. The rolls — which looked like short, moist sausages, laid side by side on the table — were taken by the second workman, and used in building up the pots.

Lawrence noticed that he worked but a few minutes on one, then went to another, and he inquired the reason.

THE MELTING-POTS.

"If I should build a pot right up from the bottom with soft clay," replied the man, "it would all sink down to the floor with its own weight. We must leave each pot to dry a little before we add much to it."

Lawrence noticed how skilfully he applied one end of a roll to the mass, and pressed it in, working it towards him, around the edge of the pot; leaving no chance for an air-bubble to hide away in it, and expand and crack the clay when afterwards subjected to heat; shaping and smoothing all with his hand, and rounding the top into a dome. The boy watched and admired, and said at length he thought it "quite an art."

The man had just pressed the end of a roll upon the back of one of his monsters, and he left it sticking out ludicrously like a tail, while he answered, "It 's no art; it 's only a notion. It takes a little gumption, and a deal of patience, — that 's all."

"I 'd rather be you up here than that man treading down stairs; you have some exercise for your wits," said Lawrence.

"I 'd sooner be the man down stairs," replied the artist. "He has no care on his mind but to hear the bell, and go to dinner. But I 'm all the while in trouble, — fearing my pots won't come out right, dreading they may crack, or something, and I 'll be shown the gate." And, seizing hold of the tail, he proceeded to work it around towards the side until it had disappeared in the mass.

"How long will such a pot as this last?"

"There 's no telling anything about it. It may crack in a week, or it may run four or five months. Two made just alike, of the same batch of clay, will act that way. There 's no help for it, but just to break 'em up and work 'em over again."

"They are like some people I know," said the Doctor, "who are always in the furnace of affliction, or being broken and trodden underfoot, and made ready for another turn at the fire. Stourbridge clay is much like human clay, after all."

"But this clay gets a little rest in here," said the gaffer. "We like to have a pot a year old before we use it. When one is wanted, we lower it on a truck through this trap door, and run it into a pot arch, which is nothing but a great oven, or kiln, where it is heated by degrees, and left about a week, and then taken out red-hot, and run into its place in an arch of one of the great furnaces."

Lawrence said he should think that must be an operation worth seeing; — a heavy pot like that, red-hot! "How much does it weigh?"

"About two thousand pounds."

"And how much does it hold?" asked the Doctor.

"Something like twenty-three hundred-weight of material," said the gaffer.

IV.

WHAT GLASS IS MADE OF.

In the yard below they found a man knocking the head out of a hogshead, which proved to be full of broken glass.

"This we buy to melt over again. Good flint glass is worth to us about two cents a pound. This cask came from New Orleans; some of it was perhaps picked up by the rag-pickers. Did you ever watch them turning over piles of rubbish, or raking the gutters with their hooks? You 'll see them carefully fish out bits of flint glass, and put them into their bags, along with old rags, old bones, and pieces of old coal. The old rags go to the paper-makers or shoddy-makers; and the old glass, and perhaps some of the old bones, come to us."

"What do you do with old bones?" asked Lawrence, seeing a large pile of them in a corner of the yard.

"We use many different substances in making different kinds of glass. We use bones — or phosphate of lime, which is what bones are mostly composed of — in making opaque white glass. Now come into the cullet-room."

"Cullet? — what is cullet?"

The gaffer showed two old women sorting over heaps of broken glass, and said "That is cullet."

"Where did you ever get such a name?"

The gaffer could not tell. But the Doctor said it was probably the French *cueillette* (from the same root as our word *cull*), meaning a gathering, a picked-up lot, a *collection* (also from the same root), and said he thought it applied very aptly to such a curious heap.

"A vast quantity accumulates about a glass-factory," said the gaffer. "Sometimes you would think more than half goes into the waste-pans, when we are blowing. But nothing is wasted. As the old, burnt-out pots are good to mix with fresh clay in making new ones, so cullet, melted over again with the other materials, improves the quality of the product. Now for the other materials."

"What! do you use sugar?" said Lawrence, as they came to a number of upright open barrels.

"Taste it," said the gaffer.

"Sand!" exclaimed Lawrence, the moment his fingers touched it. "But don't it look like pulverized white sugar? Where do you get it?"

"From Berkshire County. It is washed there, and put up wet, to prevent it from sifting out of the barrels. Here we are drying it in this sand-oven," — and the gaffer showed a heap spread out on a large, pan-shaped table, heated from beneath. "Sand," he added, "is the principal article in the manufacture of flint glass."

"Why do you call it *flint?*"

"In the English factories," said the gaffer, "it used to be made of flint stone, broken up and ground. But in this country glass-makers found sand much easier to be obtained. They got it at first from Demerara, in South America; homeward-bound ships brought it as ballast. But the War of 1812 interfered with commerce, and compelled them to look at home for their sand, as for many other things. At first they used the sand of Plymouth Beach, until better was found at Morris River, in New Jersey. But a few years ago sand of the first quality turned up in Berkshire County. This is almost pure silica. Silica is the article required, whether it occurs in flint or sand."

"And what do you put with it to make glass?"

"You can make glass of two materials, — silica and an alkali. But it is good for nothing. It has no solidity. It will dissolve in hot water. To give it density and hardness, we add either lime, or — this material."

"Red sand?" said Lawrence. "No, this is n't sand!" — putting his hand into the barrel. "What is it?"

"Red-lead," said the Doctor.

"Ground and sifted, ready for use," added the gaffer. "It is not ground fine, like the red-lead painters use. This or litharge — which is another form of almost the same substance, and answers the same purpose — is used in making flint glass.

"But what *is* red-lead? What is it made of?"

"It is made of common lead, such as you run bullets out of. You 've noticed, in melting it, that a thin skin always forms on the lead, which you call dross, and throw away? That is a result of the mixture of the oxygen of the air with the lead it comes in contact with; that is, so much of the lead is *oxidized.* It is on its way to become litharge, or red-lead, which is lead oxidized to the highest degree. To make the oxide, they melt lead on the floor of a large oven. It becomes a bright lake of melted metal, at first; it is stirred, and kept burning, until the last appearance of anything like liquid lead is worked out of it. Some glass-factories make their own red-lead; but ours comes from Galena, in just this shape, as you see it."

"In what proportion do you mix your materials for flint glass?"

"Three parts of sand, two of red-lead, and one of alkali, is about as simple a statement as I can make of it. That will make you good strong glass. But there will be a tinge of green in it, such as you see in a pane of common window-glass if you look across the edge of it. That comes from a minute quantity of iron which is contained even in the purest silica. A little arsenic and oxide of manganese take it out, or, as we say, decolorize it. Too much lead gives a yellowish cast to the glass. The oxides of other metals are used to give different colors. In making different kinds of glass, the materials may be varied indefinitely. Boracic acid may take the place of silica. Oxide of zinc may take the place of red-lead; in window and plate glass, lime takes its place. A variety of other substances are used to produce certain effects. But the common transparent glass-ware used in every house is the kind we call flint, and it is composed of the materials I have named, — silica, oxide of lead, and the alkalies, with arsenic and oxide of manganese to decolorize it."

"What do you use for alkalies?" asked the Doctor.

"Pearlash and saltpetre, or pearlash and soda. Here is where we purify the saltpetre."

The gaffer showed a tank, the bottom and sides of which were thickly incrusted with beautiful large crystals. "The saltpetre," he explained, "is dissolved in hot water. The liquid is skimmed, and allowed to cool. As the crystals form, they exclude all impurities, which are drained off with the remaining liquid. The pearlash is purified in a different way. It is dissolved, like the saltpetre; but the impurities, except what are skimmed off, settle to the bottom, in what we call slurry, which we sell to chemical works. The liquid is then evaporated in these large caldrons, until only the dry, clear pearlash remains."

The gaffer then showed where the several materials were all thrown together into a tank, and mixed. "They are then ready to be loaded upon this carriage, and taken to the blowing-house, — which we will now go and see."

This was delightful news to Lawrence, who was getting tired of these preliminaries, and eager to witness the wonders of blowing and working the melted material.

V.

THE GLASS-BLOWERS.

THE gaffer led the way into a spacious building, full of strange lights and flames and human life. Furnaces were glowing; men and boys were at work before the fires, or darting to and fro; some were blowing fiery bubbles, which put to shame all the soap-bubbles in the world; others were shaping the glowing metal; there were noises like the reports of pocket-pistols, and sounds of clanging iron, where boys were knocking off cold glass from the ends of iron rods into small sheet-iron carriages.

Altogether the scene was so dazzling and confusing that Lawrence at first thought there was little chance of his learning any more about glass-making here than he knew already. First, one had a bubble, then another had it; then it had disappeared, and the man who he thought had it was quietly at work on a lamp-chimney or a goblet, while he knew no more how he came by it than if it had been produced by magic.

"It is magic!" he exclaimed.

"That was, in old times, the popular notion with regard to glass-making; and I believe glass-blowers rather favored the superstition," said the Doctor.

"They used to dress in the skins of beasts, to protect themselves from the heat, when they were setting pots in the furnaces," said the gaffer; "and they wore great blue or green goggles on their eyes; and sometimes, after the job was done, and they wanted a good time, — glass-blowers have always been rather fond of a good time, — they would rush out into the village in their outlandish rig, and frighten the natives, like so many demons."

"But they were a superstitious class themselves," said the Doctor. "They believed in the salamander, which was supposed to be generated by the flames of a furnace that had been kept burning a great while, and to live in them. When any workman disappeared mysteriously, the salamander was supposed to have rushed out and caught him, and carried him into his den. Or was it only a joke of theirs, gaffer?"

"The worst salamander that ever carried off a glass-blower was the fiery monster we call rum," said the gaffer. "A good many have been carried off by that, and I guess that is what they meant."

"Glass-makers have had the reputation of being hard drinkers; why is it?" said the Doctor.

"They are a hard-working class; but their work is irregular. They have plenty of money, and plenty of leisure time to spend it, — a dangerous circumstance for a man or a boy, in or out of the glass-house," added the gaffer, with a look at Lawrence. "But glass-makers have improved in this respect of late years. Look around you; have n't we a pretty respectable set of men at work here?"

While the Doctor was looking at the men, Lawrence took a general view of the building. He counted four separate furnaces. Two were on one side, and seemed to be merely large ovens with flaming mouths. These he was told were the "leers" where the newly made glass-ware was annealed. Then near each end of the building, standing by the great chimneys, like dwarfs beside giants, were two small round furnaces, blazing at several mouths, called "glory-holes," at which men and boys appeared constantly heating and reheating articles of glass to be worked.

The great chimneys themselves, however, were what most astonished Lawrence. They resembled circular brick towers, with port-holes of fire; their tops disappearing through the high, broad-arched, strongly raftered roof. Into the port-holes men were thrusting iron rods, and taking out lumps of melted metal, and shaping them on tables, or blowing them into globes, or dropping them into moulds. "These then," he thought, "are the big furnaces; and those port-holes must be the necks of the melting-pots."

"We are now standing right over the cave," said the gaffer. "This furnace has eleven arches; the other has eight; and in each arch is set one of these pots, such as you saw. The crown of the furnace is built over them, so as to reflect the heat down on to them, and the flues carry it all around them. Look in and see the melted metal."

Lawrence, shielding his eyes with his hand, advanced to one of the port-holes, and saw what seemed a pot of liquid fire within, of intensely dazzling brightness.

"How long does it take to melt down your raw materials to that shape?" he asked, drawing back, with flushed face.

"We don't fill a pot all at once," said the gaffer. "We put in about a quarter or a third of a charge at a time; then, when that melts, another lot. When the pots are full, they are closed up, and we push the fires; the materials are fused and mixed by a sort of boiling caused by the escape of carbonic acid gas. When the materials are of poor quality, a sort of scum, called sandiver, or glass-gall, rises to the top, and must be skimmed off. The metal is *fined,* as we say, by keeping it for forty or fifty hours at a much higher temperature than when we finally begin to work it. After the bubbles are all out of it, and it has become what we call *plain,* that is, clear glass, we let it cool a little, regulating the fires so as to keep it in the best condition for working. It requires a deal of care and judgment to get it right every time. We blow four days in the week. Friday and Saturday we clear up, fill the pots, set a new one, if one has been broken, and get ready for the next week's blowing. Sunday night the glass in the pots is plain; and at one o'clock the first set of hands come on."

"In the night? how do you like that?" Lawrence asked a workman who was lighting his pipe of tobacco with a piece of red-hot glass.

"Well enough," said the man. "I does my work and I gits my sleep. We works from one o'clock at night till six in the morning, then we goes home and to bed, and t' other set of hands comes on. We comes on again at one in the afternoon, and works till six in the evening; then t' other set takes our place, and works till midnight."

"How does the work agree with you? I could n't stand the heat," said Lawrence, retreating still farther from the furnace.

"Glass-blowers is as healthy and long-lived as any class of men," was the reply. "I never takes cold, though some does."

So saying, the workman, having lighted his short clay pipe, took his long iron pipe, — it was, perhaps, five feet long and an inch in diameter, — and thrust one end of it into the neck of a pot, and commenced turning it.

"That is what we call gathering," said the gaffer.

When the workman had got what he judged to be a sufficient quantity of the melted metal on the end of the iron, — it was a lump somewhat larger than a butternut, — he took it out, and rolled it on a small, polished iron table, which the gaffer said was a *marver*.

"A corruption of *marbre*, the French word for marble," said the Doctor. "The English workmen got a good many terms from the French and Italians, along with their trade. The marver used to be made of marble or stone, did n't it, gaffer? and the name has gone over to the iron slab."

The workman, having reduced the soft lump to a shape suitable for his purpose, put the other end of

PREPARING TO BLOW.

the pipe to his lips, and began to blow. Lawrence, watching closely, could see a little bubble of air push out into the lump, which at the same time began to swell into a bulb. The man continued to blow, and the lump continued to expand. Now he held it down near the floor, and swung it to and fro, still blowing at intervals, and increasing its size, while the motion stretched it until it had become a large bulb with a long neck. Then he touched the end to the ground, to prevent it from expanding farther in that direction; in the mean while the thin glass of the neck had become cool, and ceased to enlarge; so that now, when he blew again, the thicker and softer glass of the sides of the bulb swelled out into a more spherical form. It was now shaped something like a small gourd, hanging by its straight stem from the end of the pipe, and the glass, which had been at a white heat at first, had become transparent at the neck, and a dull lurid red in the bulb. The workman now took an instrument in his hand, and pinched the thick soft glass at the extremity of the bulb into a button, like a blow at the end of the gourd.

All this was done in scarcely more than a minute's time; and Lawrence was amused to observe that the blower, while producing these magical effects with his iron pipe, had never once taken the clay pipe out of his mouth.

"How can you blow and smoke at the same time?" he asked, as the man stood twirling his glass gourd in the air, waiting for a boy to come and take it. "I should think you would blow the smoke and tobacco out of your pipe."

"O, I just claps my tongue over the end on 't, and stops the hole, when I blows," was the answer.

A boy now ran up and took the iron tube with the glass on its end. Lawrence followed him, convinced that the only way of learning how any article was made was to watch it from the beginning through each stage of the process.

The boy handed it to a workman sitting on a chair-shaped bench with strong, straight arms, across which he laid the iron, with the glass at his right hand. Turning the rod, by rolling it under his left hand, like a lathe, he gave the button another pinch, and then knocked it off. The end of the gourd now had a small hole in it.

"Notice the instrument he uses," said the gaffer.

"It. looks like a pair of sheep-shears," said Lawrence, "only the blades are duller. What do you call it?"

"The old name, *pucellas*, has about gone out of use with us. We call it simply a pair of *tools*. They are, pre-eminently, the glass-blower's *tools*, — he shapes everything with them."

The workman in the mean while had handed the pipe back to the boy, who thrust the glass into the flames of one of the "glory-holes."

"It is coal tar that gives that hot flash," said the gaffer. "In the other glory-hole furnace, over yonder, we burn rosin. He is heating the glass again, so that it can be shaped."

It was but the work of a few moments; and the glass was handed, glowing, back to the workman, who had in the mean while taken the button off from another precisely similar glass, which had been handed him by another boy. This he now exchanged for the first. He laid the pipe across the arms of his bench, as before, and, turning it rapidly under his hand, pushed the point of one blade of his sheep-shears, or "tools," into the hole left by the knocked-off button. Having opened it a little, he inserted both points, and gradually enlarged the hole, now to the size of a penny, now to that of a dollar, and lastly to that of a little tin cap that he fitted to a rim, which, in working, he had turned outward upon the edge of the glass. He used the cap as a measure, and it was laid aside when the rim was found to be of the right circumference. It was less than a minute's work, and that end of the gourd was finished. But it was no longer a gourd; it was a lamp-chimney.

Another boy now came forward with another iron rod, closely resembling the blowing-pipe, except that it had no hole through it.

"That is what we call a *ponty* or *pontil*," said the gaffer.

On the end of the ponty was a little wheel of red-hot glass. Applied to the bottom of the lamp-chimney, it fitted the opening. The workman then touched the top of the chimney, where it joined the blowing-pipe, with cold steel, and cracked it off. The chimney was then taken away, sticking to the glass wheel on the end of the ponty.

"That is what we call *reversing* it," said the gaffer.

The top of the chimney was now heated at the glory-hole, as the bottom had previously been, and afterwards, when soft, smoothed and shaped by the workman. This done, he gave the opposite end of the ponty a gentle knock, and the chimney fell off from the little glass wheel. One boy took it up on a stick, and placed it in a box packed nearly full of chimneys; while another reheated the glass wheel at the end of the ponty, and a third carried a blowing-pipe to one of the little sheet-iron carriages, or "pans," and knocked off the cold glass left by the last article that had been blown upon it.

Lawrence now watched another blower. He gathered on his pipe a larger lump of metal than the first, rounded it on a marver, and blew it into a surprisingly large and beautiful bubble, which put on all the colors of the dying dolphin, as the light shone upon its cooling surface. He held it down and swung it, to lengthen it; or he held it above his head, to flatten it at the poles; he whirled it, to perfect the sphere; he pinched a button out of the thick soft glass that seemed forming into a large drop at the end of it; and finally exchanged it, pipe and all, for a clean pipe, with which he proceeded to blow another.

A second workman then took the bubble, knocked off the button, and fashioned it very much as his fellow had fashioned the lamp-chimney. But, instead of coming out of his hands a lamp-chimney, it came out a beautiful, large lamp-globe. This a boy took, and hastened with it to one of the leers, or annealing ovens.

A third was blowing a small balloon of glass, giving to it gradually the form of a cylinder,— flattening the end by spatting it down smartly upon a marver on the ground. When reversed on a ponty, it was so large and heavy, and it swayed and staggered so, that Lawrence thought surely it would break off and fall. But the boy who had it, by skilfully balancing it, and turning the ponty, kept it on, until the glass had hardened sufficiently to remain in position, while he heated the opposite end at a glory-hole. This being shaped, the article turned out to be a glass jar of large size.

In surprising contrast with this was the making of that most exquisite of all drinking-vessels, the small, delicate wineglass.

"Watch these two men," said the gaffer.

One was blowing a thick bubble no bigger than a thimble; the other was blowing one somewhat larger.

"They are both at work on one glass. This larger bubble is to be the bowl. Now look."

The blower drew out the soft metal from the end of the bubble into a slender stem. The other blower now brought his smaller bubble, stuck the

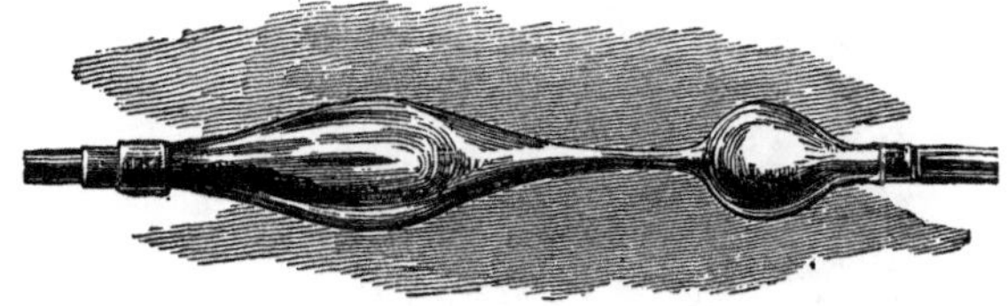

bottom of it to the end of the stem, and then by a touch of cold steel, cracked it off from his pipe. The chief blower now had at the end of his pipe two bubbles, with a stem between them, and with a hole in the end of the outer and smaller bubble. This, softened at the furnace door, was not only opened by the tools, but turned completely inside out, and flattened into a perfect little wheel on the end of the stem, thus becoming the foot of the wineglass.

The glass was then reversed on a ponty, and taken to a third workman, with now a hole in the larger bubble, where it, in its turn, had been cracked off from the pipe. This hole was enlarged by the tools, and the rough edge of the soft glass trimmed off with a pair of scissors, as a tailor would trim a bit of cloth. The half-closed bowl was then held in the furnace until it seemed soft and tremulous as melting wax, and was thrown open to its proper wineglass shape simply by the centrifugal force given to it by the ponty whirled in the workman's skilful fingers. A few light touches afterwards, and the article was per-

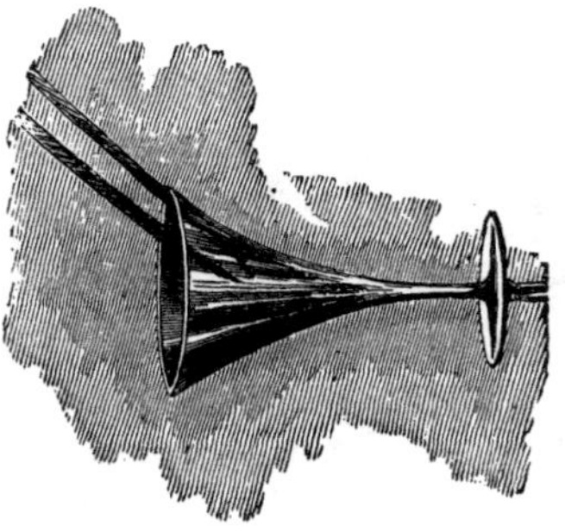

fected, — as delicate and graceful a little gem of a glass as could be made anywhere in the world.

"There, Doctor!" said the gaffer, "you might give

the remainder of your natural life to the business and you could never do that! That man began to work in glass when he was a boy, and it has become second nature with him, like speaking his native language. He has handled the blowing-pipe and the ponty until they are like parts of his own hands. He almost *feels* the glass on the end of them."

The Doctor expressed his suprise at the quickness of the operation, and the simplicity and cheapness of the tools employed.

"All the tools he uses," rejoined the gaffer, "do not cost more than fifteen dollars, and they will last him his life."

"What is this?" said Lawrence, picking up a piece of glass from the floor. "It looks like a broken thermometer-tube."

"It was blown for one," said the gaffer.

"Blown?—so small!" exclaimed Lawrence. "I can't find any hole in it."

"It has a hole—or *bore*, as we call it—of the usual size; but it is flat. That is to make a very little mercury look to be a good deal. Do you see a narrow white strip running the length of the tube?"

Lawrence saw it, and said he had often observed the stripe in the backs of thermometers, but had never learned what it was for.

"It is a background to see the mercury against. Would you like to see such a tube made? Come here. Watch this man."

With delight and curiosity Lawrence watched. The man was gathering a lump of metal from one of the pots. He blew into it gently, and shaped it on a marver, flattening it until it resembled in form and size the part of a sword-hilt that is grasped by the hand.

"In flattening it," said the gaffer, "he flattened the bubble of air he had blown into it." Lawrence looked, and could see the bubble, about as broad as his finger, extending through the glass. "That is to be the bore of the thermometer,—though of itself it is now larger than two or three thermometer tubes. Now they are going to put on the stripe."

A boy brought a lump of melted, opaque white glass on a ponty. It was touched to the now hardened sword-hilt, and drawn from end to end along the flat side, leaving a stripe about as broad as a lady's finger. The sword-hilt, with the stripe carefully pressed down and hardened upon it, was now plunged into a pot of melted glass, and thickly coated; the soft exterior was rounded on a marver, until the entire body of glass, enclosing the stripe and the flattened bore, was in size and shape a little longer and considerably larger than a banana.

This was now slowly heated to a melting state. Then came forward a boy with a ponty, bearing on its end a piece of glass resembling an inverted conical inkstand. This he set upright on the ground, the bottom of the inkstand uppermost. The blower, with the melting lump, now advanced, and held it over the ponty, until the soft mass drooped down and touched the bottom of the inkstand, to which it adhered. The man and the boy held the lump a moment between them; then, at a word of command, the boy shouldered his ponty, like a very large staff with a very small bundle on the end of it, and set out to travel. As he ran in one direction, into a work-room, the man backed off in the other, the glowing lump stretching between them, like some miraculous kind of spruce gum. In a minute they were seventy or eighty feet apart, with a gleaming cord of glass, smaller than a pipe-stem, sagging between them. This was presently lowered, laid out at its full length upon the ground, and broken from what was left of the lump at the ends.

Even the Doctor, who had hitherto said little, now expressed his astonishment and admiration, exclaiming, "It is marvellous! it is truly marvellous!"

"Of course," said the gaffer, "the bore stretches with the tube, and keeps its flattened shape. So does the stripe."

"But what keeps the tube of uniform size? Why don't it break?" said Lawrence.

"The reason is this. As the glass runs out thin, it cools, and stops stretching, while it continues to draw out the soft glass from the thicker parts at the ends. If we wish to make a small tube, we stretch it quick, without giving it much time to cool. To make a large tube, we stretch slower. Here is a piece of barometer tubing, stretched in the same way; so is this lot of homœopathic medicine vials." The "vials" were a small stack of hollow glass canes, about five feet in length, standing in a corner of the work-room, into which the visitors had followed the boy. "Though, of course," added the gaffer, "to make them, we don't flatten the bore, but only blow it larger."

"Then how are vials made out of these tubes?"

"They are cut into pieces of the right length, then the bottoms are melted and closed in by means of a common blow-pipe, such as chemists use."

Lawrence was about to ask a similar question with regard to the thermometers, when a man came along, and, stooping, commenced cutting the long tube into uniform lengths of about five feet, and packing them together into a narrow, long box.

"These," said the gaffer, "he sends to his shop in Boston, — for he is a thermometer-maker; there they are cut up into tubes of the right length; an end of each one is melted and blown out into a bulb, — the tube itself serving as a very small blowing-pipe. To avoid getting moisture into the bulb, air from a small india-rubber bag is used, instead of breath from the mouth. As the bag is squeezed at one end, the bulb swells at the other."

"Then how is the mercury put in? So small a bore!" said Lawrence, trying to find it with a pin point.

"The glass is heated, and that expands the air in it, and expels the greater part of it. As the air that is left cools and contracts, it is made to suck in the mercury. To expel the rest of the air, the mercury is boiled in the tube. When there is enough mercury in the tube to fill it, at as high a degree of temperature as it is expected ever to go, the end is softened, bent over, and closed up. As the mercury cools and contracts, it leaves a vacuum at the upper part of the tube."

As Lawrence stood aside to make room for the boy, who was stretching another eighty-foot tube, the gaffer continued: —

"Glass beads and bugles are made in much the same way. Glass of any desired color is used. It is blown, and stretched into tubes a hundred feet long or more. These are broken up into bits of the right length for the required bead. To make a round bead, the bits are put into a sort of mud, made of sand and ashes, and worked about in it till the holes are filled up. They are afterward put into a heated cylinder, along with sand; the cylinder is made to revolve, and the motion, with the friction of the sand, wears down the edges of the softened glass till the beads become round, — the sand and ashes in them preventing the sides from flattening."

VI.

MOULDING AND PRESSING.

THE gaffer now took his visitors around to another side of the blowing-room, and showed them the process of blowing glass into a mould. This was of cast-iron, and worked by a boy, who opened and shut it by means of handles. The blower gathered the melted glass, rolled it on a marver, blew into it slightly, then dropped it, in a long, purse-shaped, glowing lump, into the open mould. This was immediately closed by the boy; then the blower blew until a bubble, pushed up on the top of the mould, expanded to the size of a football, and to the thinness of the thinnest transparent film, and finally burst with a loud pop, flying into shreds of tinsel, light as feathers. The mould was then opened, and a caster-vial with figured sides was exposed. This was taken up by a second boy on a "snap-dragon," — a rod something like a ponty, but with a socket at the end for holding articles of glass, — and carried to a glory-hole, where the round, open top was heated. It was then passed to a workman seated in a chair, who shaped the top, and pressed into it a piece of iron called a "lip-maker." The top was then a mouth, and the vial became a "vinegar," as the boys called it. Another man was blowing "mustards," in the same way; and a third was blowing "inks."

"Does it blow easy?" Lawrence inquired of the last.

"It don't require much effort," said the man; and, having his glass all ready to drop, he put the pipe into Lawrence's hand, who lowered the stretching, purse-shaped lump into the mould, and blew. He blew till a bubble sprang up on the top of the mould, and cracked like a pistol: then with a laugh gave back the pipe to the man. The mould was opened, and a nice little inkstand came out.

"You shall keep that to remember us by," said the gaffer. "But don't touch it yet!" — as Lawrence was about to handle it. "It's hissing hot! I'll mark it so we shall know it again."

This done he took up a handful of the glass tinsel from a heap formed by the breaking bubbles, crushed it, threw it in the air, and said, as it fell in a glittering shower, "This is the diamond dust ladies powdered their hair with a few years ago."

As they passed on, he continued: "You have now seen the two processes by which blown glass is made, — the simple blowing, which is as ancient as the time of Moses, and the modern process of blowing into moulds. Here is something else."

A workman, who had gathered some metal, dropped it, without blowing at all, into an elaborately constructed mould, the several parts of which were opened and closed by means of at least half a dozen handles. The soft, glowing glass being securely shut into it, the mould was shoved under a strong hand-press, and a plunger brought down forcibly into it by a man at the lever. The plunger being lifted, and the mould opened, a cream-pitcher appeared, with the handle, all complete.

"This," said the gaffer, "is what we call *pressing*. It is claimed by some as an American invention. Whether it is or not, it is quite modern, and it has been carried to a higher degree of perfection in this country than anywhere else. Here is a press that is making a large preserve-dish, elaborately figured, a really elegant article. It is done, you see, almost in a moment. Here is another man working two different moulds, and turning out two hundred small preserve-plates in a minute. You can see by this how much the use of moulds must have done towards cheapening the price of glass. And, really," he added, "we are making pressed glass nowadays that is almost as clear and beautiful as blown, — though of course there is a popular prejudice in favor of the blown article, since it is more expensive."

Lawrence asked a workman who was cutting off the melted glass from the ponty, as it dropped into a mould, if it "cut easy."

"Well, about as easy as stiff dough cuts. Try it."

And Lawrence, applying the shears, clipped off a lump, which, pressed in the mould, came out a graceful goblet.

VII.

PLATING AND ANNEALING.

"Now," said the gaffer, "I believe you have seen about everything."

"No," said Lawrence; "I have n't seen how you make glass of two different colors, — a lamp-shade, for instance, which is all red, perhaps, except where there are figures of transparent glass."

"Let me see," said the gaffer, looking about him. "We are not doing any plating to-day. But we will do some, to show you."

Lawrence begged he would not give himself any trouble.

"That is what I shall say when I go to visit you some time. 'Don't give yourself any trouble for me,' I shall say to your aunt. But she will give herself trouble, and I trust it will be a pleasure for her to do so. Now I must give myself trouble, to show you how glass-plating is done; and it will be a pleasure."

He gave orders to some men, who stopped the work they were at to assist him. A piece of hard ruby glass, previously prepared, was melted on the end of a ponty; two soft lumps of it were taken off on the ends of two blowing-pipes, — "for I am going to show you two different ways of plating," said the gaffer. "I am going to make two ruby cups. To save the colored glass, which is costly, we put a thin plate of it on a body of flint glass. This lump I shall put on the outside of the first cup. The lump on the other pipe will go on the inside of the second cup. Now look sharp.

He blew the first lump into a bowl-like shape. "This," said he, "is the shell." It was broken off, and placed in a secure position on the ground, with the opening uppermost. Then a lump of soft flint-glass was brought, of which the gaffer blew a bubble into the ruby shell until it filled it. The mouth of the shell was then closed in upon the flint, and the two completely welded into one hollow globe. This was now made thoroughly soft at the fire, blown, reversed, opened at the end, trimmed with scissors about the edges, and finally shaped into a cup. But it had no handle. The melted piece of ruby was accordingly brought again, touched to the top of what was to be the back of the cup, stretched out, and a stick three or four inches long, resembling a stick of soft, stretching, bright red candy, clipped off. This, adhering to the top of the cup, was stretched upward an inch or two farther, then bent backward, curved inward, and pressed to the back of the cup near the bottom. One or two little touches to give it a graceful form, and the handle was finished.

He kept the second cup along in nearly the same stages of shaping as the first, working on one while his assistants were reheating the other. The process of shaping was the same with each. But the process of plating the second on the inside was much simpler and easier. The lump of ruby was immersed in melted flint, coated with it, and then blown.

"Why don't you do all your plating in that way?" asked Lawrence.

"We do, unless we wish to produce the effect you have noticed on the lamp-shades. For that the ruby must be on the outside. The transparent figures are cut through it into the clear glass, — as you will see when you visit the cutting-room."

The gaffer then presented the two cups to Lawrence, — one for himself, and one for his little cousin at home.

"But," said he, "they must be annealed before you can take them."

"What is annealing?"

"Come this way," said the gaffer. "This is the leer. Look in."

Lawrence looked in through the wreaths of thin, undulating flames that poured out of the mouth of the oven, or flowed away in graceful waves and curves under the long, low vault within, and saw a thickly clustered row of glass articles stretching far away towards an opening where daylight shone at the opposite end of the leer.

"Here are four leers," said the gaffer, "two on each side of this passage. From this end, where the glass goes in, to the other, where it is taken out, the distance is eighty feet. The glass is placed on pans, which are hooked together; so that, when one is drawn forward at the other end, that draws the whole string forward. When a pan is emptied at that end, it is sent back, and hooked on and filled again at this

THE LEER.

end. There is your little inkstand, beginning its journey in grand company, — fruit-dishes, and ruby and blue lamp-shades, which look pretty enough under the rolling flames. I'll put your ruby cups near them, and leave directions at the other end with the man who will take them out: he will bring them to me."

"How long will it take them to go through?"

"About twenty-four hours. The fire is at this end of the oven. As the articles pass through, they cool very slowly, and come out almost cold at the other end. In this way we give the particles of glass time to get acquainted, and to nestle together comfortably and contentedly before they harden. That makes them fast friends. Your cups and inkstand would be apt to break the first time you used them if they were not annealed."

"I see you send nearly everything to the leers, except the lamp-chimneys," said the Doctor.

"Yes. The thinner the glass the less liable it is to crack from exposure to heat and cold. The lamp-chimneys are of such uniform thinness throughout that we don't consider it necessary to anneal them."

"I advise you to anneal them," said the Doctor. "I believe we have cracked half a dozen in my house within a week or two, and we are getting tired of them. I am quietly reading my newspaper of an evening, when — snap! — another broken chimney."

"That's because you don't buy your chimneys of us," said the gaffer, laughing.

VIII

CUTTING AND ORNAMENTING.

WALKING through the passage between the leers, they entered what is called the "sloar-room," where the glass was taken from the pans and put into boxes, to be sent up to the cutting-room.

"You must go up there now," the gaffer said to Lawrence. "As it is a separate department from mine, I will just go up and introduce you to the foreman and leave you. This way; we may as well ride."

He stepped on what appeared to be a trap-door, supported by strong uprights. Lawrence and his uncle stepped on beside him. A bar was put up, and they were enclosed in a little square pen. The gaffer then pulled a lever beside one of the uprights, and the trap-door, little square pen, passengers and all, began to ascend towards an opening in the floor overhead; having reached the level of which it stopped, the bar was let down, and Lawrence and his companions stepped off in the midst of the cutting-room.

This was a long, large room, full of whirling wheels and the sound of grinding. Overhead, running the entire length of the building, was a power-shaft, which, with its many wheels and bands, set in motion a second range of wheels below, and at these a long line of workmen and workwomen were grinding various articles of glass. Over this lower range of wheels was a row of queer-looking, tunnel-shaped wooden tubs, called hoppers, set in a strong framework, and filled with water, or with sand and water, which dripped upon the wheels.

The Doctor, looking at his watch, and remembering the business which had brought him to the vicinity of the glass-house, departed with the gaffer; and Lawrence was left with the foreman of the cutting-room.

"But where do you *cut* the glass?" the boy inquired; for he had expected to see diamonds employed in the operation.

"What is commonly called *glass-cutting*," replied the foreman, — a very obliging elderly person in shirt-sleeves and white apron, — "is nothing but *grinding* in some shape. Cutting with diamonds is a very different thing: we don't do anything of that kind here.

"Regular glass-cutting," he continued, "is done by three processes. Here is the first."

He showed a man working at a wheel wet with sand and water dripping from its companion hopper. The wheel was of iron, and the sand made a sharp, rough grit upon it. To this the man held with firm hands the stem of a goblet, very much as a knife is held to a grindstone. The stem was round as it came from the hands of the blower, and he was grinding it into angles.

"You notice," said the foreman, "that the edge of the wheel is shaped for the kind of work it is doing.

We use iron and sand first, because they cut faster than anything else. But you see how rough they leave the surface. Now see the second process. This wheel is of fine stone, and only water drips on it from the hopper. This man takes the glass as the other leaves it, and grinds off the rough surface. But it still has a dull look, as you see; and that brings us to the third process. Here the dull surface is polished on a wooden wheel, with pumice-stone and water. For the finest work, a cork wheel is used, with what we call putty, — a paste composed of lead and tin."

"Hallo!" said Lawrence, "this is what I wanted to see!" as he found a man finishing round facets that had been cut through the thin colored shell of a ruby lamp-shade into the transparent glass beneath.

The foreman was now called away, and Lawrence was left to wander about as he pleased. He watched for a long time a number of men cutting caster-bottles, wondering at the rapidity with which they turned them from angle to angle on the stones. He saw one man fitting glass stoppers to decanters, — a simple process by which they were made air-tight. The stopper, set fast in a lathe, was set whirling, and ground down roughly at first with a piece of sheet-iron in sand and water. It was then inserted in the neck of the decanter, and ground on that until it fitted. Three or four workmen were cutting stars in the bottoms of preserve-dishes, while others were simply taking off the rough spot left by the ponty on the bottoms of articles that had been blown.

At one end of the room some women were at work on transparent lamp-globes, which had come up from below in a large packing-box. A globe was taken, attached to a lathe, and set whirling over a trough half filled with sand and water. In one hand the workwoman held a stiff wire brush, which she pressed upon the glass, while she applied to it sand and water, in profuse quantities, dipped up from the trough with the other hand. In this way she ground thoroughly the glass about the two ends of the globe, rendering it white and opaque, but leaving a broad belt about the centre untouched. She then stopped the lathe, took off the globe and rinsed it, showing the polar regions, so to speak, white with frost, which extended well down into the temperate zones, while the torrid zone remained crystal clear. She told Lawrence the process was called "roughing."

He followed the globes from her hands to those of a workman sitting at a narrow-edged grindstone, on which he was ornamenting the transparent space between the ground parts. Now he was cutting buds and petals, now leaves, and now a waving stem surrounding the globe like a tipsy equator, uniting the whole in a graceful garland of flowers. His cuts on the glass were not afterwards polished, but were left white and opaque.

Lawrence asked if he called his work engraving.

"It is a sort of coarse engraving; but we call it simply cutting," replied the man. "The real engraving is done at the upper end of the room."

CUTTING A LAMP-GLOBE.

Thither Lawrence went, and saw the difference; yet the engraving, too, was only a species of grinding. The engraver sat on a high stool before a swiftly whirling little copper wheel, not more than two inches in diameter. To the edge of this he touched occasionally a mixture of oil and emery, in a little shallow dish, then pressed firmly upon it the article he was engraving.

He was ornamenting the sides of goblets and wine-glasses. On one he was cutting an initial letter, encircled by a delicate wreath. Lawrence asked if he had a pattern to go by.

"I make my own patterns, and carry them in my head mostly," replied the artist. "For this design, I just make four marks for the top and bottom of the letter. The wreath I do without making any marks first."

As the side he was engraving was necessarily held from him, and he could see where he was cutting only by looking *through* the glass from the other side, Lawrence wondered how he could do such fine work. The artist, seeing him interested, showed him still finer specimens. One was a fairy-like goblet, the surface of which was surrounded and filled up by the gracefully bending sprigs and drooping flowers of the fuchsia. Another was a landscape, showing a hunter and his dog in natural attitudes, and a partridge rising on the wing before the uplifted gun; and there were many more equally beautiful.

"Is it possible you do all this with a wheel?"

"I use a variety of wheels. Each has an edge shaped for the kind of work it does. Here is the smallest." It was scarcely bigger than a pin-head. "I 'll show you a design — this is it — that required nine different wheels in the cutting."

"But you must understand drawing?"

"O yes. When I began as an apprentice, thirteen years ago, I was set to work at first on broken glass, making dots and lines, like a school-boy learning to write. Then I made them on whole glass which we were not very particular about. At the same time I gave my evenings to the study of drawing. I worked hard; but a man can't accomplish much in this world unless he does apply himself."

"Is it the copper wheel that cuts the glass?"

"No; it is the emery we put on the wheel."

"Do you work nights?"

"Not often. But sometimes, when we have orders we are in a hurry to get done, I take a little work home with me in the evening."

"How do you do it at home? Your lathes here go by steam-power, don't they?"

"Yes; but I have a foot-lathe at home I can do my work on, though it is harder. In some of the English factories glass-engravers use foot-lathes altogether. Labor is cheap there."

"With the exception of this ornamental work, what is the great difference between cut glass and common glass? I see they go to work and grind down the round stems and sides of blown goblets into just such shapes as they press other glass in."

"In the first place, blown glass is freer from waves and wrinkles; and the angles on cut glass are much sharper and cleaner than on pressed glass. Although," added the engraver, admiring the perfection of a pressed goblet, "they are getting to do some of their pressed work so well, that, with a little subsequent burnishing, it almost equals the cut. It is not so apt to crack as the cut glass is, besides being so much cheaper. You may usually know pressed glass by this little seam on each side, left by the crease in the moulds; though from some articles it is burnished off."

IX.

COLORING AND SILVERING.

FROM the cutting-room Lawrence found his way to the lamp-room, where he saw a number of girls at work cementing the bodies and feet of lamps together, and putting on the brass collars. Farther on he found men screwing the lamp-tops on, and fitting the metallic tops of other ware, such as pepper-boxes, "mustards," and sirup-pitchers; thence he went on to the mould-room, where the patterns were made and the moulds finished after they were brought from the foundry.

He finally inquired his way to the private room of the gaffer, whom he found sitting at a work-bench, watching what looked like a strip of copper or brass doubled up in a transparent bottle half filled with water.

"What are you doing to that old hoop?" asked Lawrence.

"That old hoop," said the gaffer, "is pure gold, enough to buy you a small farm. I am eating it up."

"Eating it up?" said Lawrence, laughing. "I don't see it."

"Eating it up with that preparation of nitric acid. Do you see it work?"

Lawrence did see, to his surprise, that the liquid was beginning to bubble about it, like some brisk sort of wine, and that the old hoop was gradually sinking down into it.

"It looks," he said, "as if the gold was on fire, and sending up fine vaporous flames through the liquor. But is n't it a poor use to put gold to? especially at the present premium."

"We use gold in coloring ruby glass; that is what makes ruby glass so expensive. We use old bones, or the phosphate of lime, as I told you, to make white glass, and the oxides of iron, copper, and silver to make other colors. The yellowish tint, with shades of green and opal, which you may have seen in Bohemian glass, is produced chiefly by uranium."

"What is stained glass, such as we read of in descriptions of old cathedral windows?"

"Staining is a kind of painting on glass. The colors are a mineral composition; and they are melted into the glass, so that nothing will ever fade them or wash them out. Fancy articles of glass are often painted in the same way."

"How is this silver glass made?" asked Lawrence, taking up a door-knob from the bench. "It looks like silver, and it always keeps bright. I have seen pitchers and sugar-bowls and lamp-reflectors made of it."

"That is a new process, but quite simple. I 'll tell

you how we make a reflector, for instance. The glass is blown into a large bubble, which is worked flat across the top, and saucer-shaped at the bottom. Then the blower puts his mouth to the pipe, but, instead of blowing, he sucks, and draws the top in until it almost touches the bottom. Then you have something like a broad, shallow dish with a lining. Here are half a dozen of them. The hole in the bottom part is caused by the cracking off of the pipe after it is blown. You see there is a narrow space between the bottom part and the lining. Now I'll show you how the silvering is done."

The gaffer took a tall measuring-glass, and went into another room, where there were some jars of transparent liquid on a shelf.

"This jar," said he, "contains nitrate of silver"; and he poured a small quantity into the glass. Then he went to another jar. "This is a solution of grape sugar, — nothing more nor less"; and he poured in a still larger quantity of that. He then went to a third jar. "This is pure water"; and he filled the glass with it.

He then turned the reflectors down on a counter, and filled the space between the bottom part and the lining of each by pouring the mixed contents of the glass in through the hole. When they were full, he took them to an oven, and placed them on a pan of hot sand.

"That is all," said he, shutting the oven. "In half an hour I come again and take them, pour out the liquid, and find that the silver in it has completely coated the inside of the glass. Pitchers and goblets are made in the same way, except that the lining, instead of being sucked in by the blower, is pushed in with a plug. After silvering, the stem and foot of the goblet are put on, and the hole in the bottom of the pitcher is closed up."

"Now I know," said Lawrence, "how those fancy glasses are made that seem to be nearly full of wine, but, when you go to drink, it turns out to be only a little wine, or some other colored liquid, under the lining. You can fool a fellow by making believe you are going to throw it in his face. Do you make window-glass here?"

"O no; blowing window-glass is another business entirely."

X.

WINDOW-GLASS AND PLATE-GLASS.

"WHAT! is window-glass blown?"

"Certainly. What is called English crown glass is made in this way. It is first blown into a large globe, then flattened and reversed on a ponty. Where the glass breaks off from the pipe, a hole is left. That side is then made melting hot before the furnace; it is whirled so swiftly that the centrifugal force given to it enlarges the hole, gradually at first, then faster and faster, then — flap! that whole side flies open, and what was a globe is a disk, or wheel, four or five feet in diameter. It is called a table. After annealing, it is cut up into panes.

"There is another process," continued the gaffer, "by which our common window-glass is made. By the way, if ever you visit Pittsburg, in Pennsylvania, you must go into the window-glass factories there; you will find them very curious. Their furnace, in the first place, is built in the ancient style: it has no chimney, and the smoke from the bituminous coal they burn pours out in a cloud into the room. There are openings in the roof for it to escape through, and a continual draught of air from the doors carries it upward, so that it is not so bad for the workmen as one would think. Besides, they do not begin to blow until the smoke is all burnt off.

"There are five pots on each side of the furnace; and you will see five men in a row, blowing all at once, with the regularity of a file of soldiers exercising. Each gathers thirty or forty pounds of metal on his pipe, which is very long and strong. They stand on platforms, to get room to swing the glass, as they blow it. The five men begin to blow and swing all together. Each blows a great globe of glass, which is stretched out gradually by the swinging motion into a cylinder, or roller, as it is called, five feet long. Then the five rollers are swung up towards the furnace-holes, and five other soldiers spring forward with their guns, — which in this case are iron bars, that they set upright under the five blowing-pipes to support them while the rollers are reheating in the necks of the pots. The blowers blow in the pipes with all their might, then clap their thumbs over the holes to prevent the air from rushing out again; in the mean while the end of the roller is softened, so that at last the air, forced in and expanded by the heat, bursts it outwards. The glass is then a cylinder, open at one end. It is whirled in the heat until the edges become true, then brought away, — the five iron supports dropping to the ground with a simultaneous clang. The cylinders are laid on tables, where the imperfect spherical end about the blowing-pipe is cracked off from the rest by a stripe of melted glass drawn around it. The cylinder is then cracked from end to end on one side by means of a red-hot iron passed through it.

"In an adjoining building is what is called the flattening oven. The cylinders brought there are lifted on the end of a lever, passed in through a circular opening just large enough to admit them, and laid on flattening stones on the oven bottom, with the crack uppermost. The oven bottom is circular, and it revolves horizontally. As the glass softens, it separates at the crack, and lays itself down gently and gradually on the stone. The long cylinder is then a flat sheet, three feet wide and nearly five feet in length. There are four openings around the sides of the oven; at one the glass is put in, through another a workman sweeps the stone for it, a third workman smooths it down with a block as it comes round to him, and a fourth, at the last opening, which is close to the one at which it was put in, lifts the sheet — partly cooled by this time — upon a carriage in the oven. This he does by means of a lever furnished with sharp, broad blades at the end, which he works in under the glass. When the carriage is full, it is run through an annealing oven beyond.

"The opposite end of the annealing oven opens into the cutting-room. There the carriages are pushed along a central track, and unloaded at the stalls of the cutters. The cutter has a table before him, with measure-marks on its edges. He lifts one of the sheets, lays it on the table, and rules it faster than a school-boy rules his slate. His ruler is a wooden rod five feet long, and his pencil-point is a diamond. Every stroke is a cut. Not that he cuts the glass quite apart; indeed, he seems scarcely to make a scratch. Yet that scratch has the effect of cracking the glass quite through, so that it breaks clean off at the slightest pressure. In this way the sheets are cut up into panes of the requisite size."

"I should think the diamonds would wear out," said Lawrence.

"I remember," replied the gaffer, "one workman told me that a single diamond would last him two or three years. It has fifteen or sixteen different edges, and when one edge is worn out, he uses another. South American diamonds, such as he used, cost, he told me, from six to thirty dollars each; and, when they are worn out for his purpose, he sells them for jewels to be put into watches."

"What is plate-glass?" Lawrence asked.

"That is not blown, but cast. The pot, or cistern, containing the melted metal, is swung up by a crane over an immense polished metallic table, and tipped. The table is heated, and there is a rim to keep the glass which is poured on from running over the sides. The glass is then rolled down to a uniform thickness by a heavy copper cylinder, reaching across the table, and resting on the rim, which is just as high as the plate is to be thick. For bow-windows the plates are bent before cutting up into panes.

"For mirrors they are silvered in this way: — A sheet of tin-foil is spread on a table, and a thin coating of mercury is poured over it. Then the glass to be silvered — sometimes an immense plate, and it has been carefully annealed, ground, and polished, of course — is slipped on in such a way as to exclude all the air from beneath it, the table being tipped just enough to let the superfluous mercury run off. When the plate is in its place on the table, it is kept for several hours under a press of heavy weights. The mercury and tin-foil combine to form what is called the amalgam, which coats the glass and makes the mirror."

XI.

OTHER CURIOUS MATTERS.

LAWRENCE said he had read that glass mirrors were modern, and that the ancients used polished metal instead. "The Romans for window-panes used sheets of mica. Yet glass-making," said he, "was a very ancient art."

"So ancient," said the Doctor, coming in just then, "that in Egypt glass ornaments have been discovered on mummies that were buried three thousand years ago; and on their monuments are still to be seen hieroglyphics, or picture writings, which represent glass-blowers at work in the same way, and with the same kinds of tools, as modern glass-blowers. The inhabitants of Tyre were famous glass-makers, after them the Romans, and after them the Venetians. It was the Venetians that introduced the art to modern Europe."

"The Germans brought it to this country," said the gaffer. "A company of them started a factory at Quincy, in Massachusetts, before the Revolution, but it did n't succeed. Mr. Hewes, a Boston merchant, next tried it. His glass-blowers were nearly all Hessians, deserters from the British army. He set up his works in the woods of New Hampshire, where fuel was cheap. But it was n't till after the beginning of the present century that glass-making began to prosper in this country. It has now become a very extensive and very profitable business. New England manufactures a good share of the flint-glass which is made in America, and which I may say, without boasting, is equal to any in the world. Our window-glass is made mostly in New Jersey, New York, and Pennsylvania. It does n't pay to manufacture that except where fuel is cheap."

"Is n't it wonderful?" said Lawrence, taking up a goblet. "In that piece of glass are white sand, and red-lead, and pearlash, and saltpetre, neither of them transparent by itself, and yet here they are all transparent! It does seem a sort of magic that has made them invisible!"

"There are many wonderful things connected with glass," said the gaffer. "It will not tarnish. Only one acid has any effect upon it. It is one of the most brittle substances, and yet one of the most elastic. A hollow glass ball can be made that will rebound half the distance to your hand if you drop it on an anvil."

Lawrence said he should like such a ball as that; but when told that it was pretty sure to break at the second or third rebound, he said "Oh!" and cheerfully gave it up.

"It makes the finest sounding bells," said the Doctor, "and musical glasses are made of it that are played by merely rubbing them with the moist fingers. It will condense moisture from the air more quickly than any of the metals."

"There is another curious thing," said the gaffer. "Drop a ball of melted glass in water, and you 'd think it would make a tremendous spluttering; but it don't at first. After it has had time to cool a little, then it sets the water to bubbling."

They had now returned to the gaffer's room, which they found so full of the fumes of the acid that Lawrence immediately began to cough.

"You see," said the gaffer, "the gold has disappeared. The acid has eaten it. Come with me now, and I'll show you something that happened while you were in the cutting-room."

Locking the door behind him, he took his visitors once more to the cave, which they found full of smoke and steam and stifling heat. There he showed them the astonishing spectacle of what seemed a cluster of icicles, some a yard in length, hanging from the grate under the big furnace.

"One of our melting-pots burst. It was nearly full of metal, which ran down into the fire. Some of it came through the grate, but the most of it rushed out through the teaze-hole in a perfect lava flood, which came near setting us on fire."

"That must have been a serious loss," said Lawrence.

"Yes. To say nothing of the pot, the glass in it was worth about a hundred and fifty dollars."

"Well," said the Doctor, "we began with the cave, and we may as well end with it." And, taking leave of the gaffer, he departed with his nephew, who, he promised, should come in a few days for the inkstand and cups.

"How wonderful it all is!" said Lawrence, as they stood on the platform, waiting for the train.

"It is truly wonderful," replied the Doctor. "When we consider the many uses to which glass is applied, its cheapness, its purity, its beauty, we find that it possesses the valuable qualities of nearly all the metals; — incorruptible as gold, clear as silver, useful as iron, what would our houses be without it? It keeps the cold out, it lets the light in. We drink out of it, and we see ourselves in it. Besides fulfilling a thousand common and domestic uses, it is made into gems that rival the brilliancy of the diamond, and into lenses which give new realms to human vision. It restores eyesight to the aged, and remedies the defective eyesight of the young. It magnifies objects invisible to the naked eye, so that they can be distinctly seen and studied; and it brings the heavens near. To it we owe our intimate acquaintance with the stars. The telescope is the father of modern astronomy, and the soul of the telescope is glass."

CHAPTER IV.

AMONG THE COAL-MINERS.

I.

A JOURNEY TO THE COAL REGION.

"WHAT are you thinking, Lawrence?" said the Doctor, as the family were seated one evening round the library fire.

October had come, the nights were growing cold, and a bright glow from the grate gave a warm and cheerful aspect to the room. The Doctor had been reading the evening paper; — Mrs. Dean was knitting a white worsted tippet, — so very white and soft that anybody would have known it was intended for Lawrence's little cousin Ethel, for where was there another little throat or chin it would become so well? Ethel was rocking pussy to sleep in her doll's cradle,—only pussy was n't very sleepy, and the sight of the white tippet was a constant temptation to her playful paws.

As for Lawrence, he was gazing abstractedly at the fire,—scarcely moving, except when, every minute or two, he took a lump of coal from the hod, and dropped it carefully into the grate, and never once speaking, for I don't know how long, until his uncle startled him with his sudden question.

"Oh! I? I was thinking how curious it is. I mean the fire. And the coal that makes the fire,—where it comes from, and how we happen to be burning it here. Ever since we saw the great furnaces at the glass-works, I can't keep it out of my head."

"No!" cried little Ethel; "he won't even look at my kitty,—and she is so interesting in her nightcap and nightgown! Only see how quiet she is! There! rock-a-by, baby, upon the tree-top! When the wind blows, the cradle will— Dear me, kitty!" she exclaimed; for there was just then an exciting movement of the white tippet, and away went kitty, nightcap, nightgown, and all, to have a snatch at it.

There was a good laugh at the funny appearance pussy made, dressed up so, with the nightcap-strings tied under her whiskers, and her paws in sleeves. And Mrs. Dean said, "You see, Ethel, cats will be cats, and boys will be boys. You must n't blame them because they won't do always just as you would like to have them. Lawrence is a good deal more interested in coal, just now, than he is in cats with nightcaps."

"For a while it was all glass," said Ethel, putting pussy back into the cradle. "There was n't a glass thing in the house that he did n't talk about, and tell us how it was made."

"Yes, and did n't you like to have me?" said Lawrence. "You made me tell you over and over again how your little ruby cup was made."

"Yes, indeed; for that is very pretty, with my initials engraved on it, and the little flower-wreath around them to match yours. But coal, — ugly black coal! — I don't see what there is interesting in that!"

"Lawrence does, and I am very glad of it," said the Doctor. "How would you like to see where the coal comes from, — eh, Lawrence?"

"That 's what I 've been wishing for!" exclaimed the boy. "If I could only go into a coal-mine!"

The good Doctor smiled. "Well, now, I 'll tell you what I have been thinking. Some gentlemen of my acquaintance talk of purchasing coal lands in Pennsylvania; and they have their eye on some near Scranton, in Luzerne County, — which you will find, when you turn to your map, about the centre of the northeastern quarter of the State. They have asked me to go out and look at this property for them, and I think of starting next week. Would you like to go with me?"

Lawrence fairly leaped out of his chair with delight. "Would I? O uncle!"

"There she goes again!" said Ethel, with a rueful face, holding pussy's nightgown in her hand, having pulled it off in a vain attempt to detain the runaway. "Why could n't you keep still, coz, when she was just getting so quiet?"

"Why, I'm going to Pennsylvania!" cried Lawrence, — as if that were excuse enough for the wildest conduct.

"Yes, but you need n't dance up and down that way, if you are! Now she won't go to sleep to-night!"

"Neither will Lawrence, I'm afraid," said his aunt. "He should n't have been told of anything so exciting until morning."

The Doctor laughed, and said, "I knew he would have to lie awake one night, thinking of it, and that may as well be to-night."

Lawrence seemed to be of the same opinion. He went to bed as usual; but he did n't want to sleep. He lay awake, thinking of the promised journey, and of coal mines and miners, for an hour or two. He was so excited, that when he fell asleep at last he dreamed that he was a locomotive in nightcap and nightgown, and that, taking fright at the sound of a gun, he ran off the track, and smashed up a long passenger train. Then it seemed to him that the noise he had taken for a gun was in fact the explosion of his own boiler; then, that he was the engineer, and that he was knocked very high by repeated explosions, which would n't let him come down out of the freezing weather. He awoke, in the midst of his trouble, to find that he had thrown off the bedclothes, that he was shivering with the cold, and that a window-blind was slamming.

The days seemed very long to the boy, until at last the time came for bidding his aunt and cousin good by, and starting with his uncle on their journey.

They took the steamboat train for New York; and Lawrence, after sleeping soundly "as a top," as he said, "on that pantry-shelf," — meaning the berth in the state-room,— awoke the next morning in the great city.

He had a few hours to look about him, while his uncle transacted some business; then they crossed the river in a ferry-boat, (how keenly the boy enjoyed all that!) and, taking a train on the other side, rattled away, across New Jersey, and far up into Pennsylvania, reaching Scranton the same evening.

It was, of course, a delightful journey to the boy, and he was almost sorry when it came to an end. Yet the end was the most interesting part of it. The train went winding in among the mountains that enclose the Lackawanna Valley; they were covered with wild forests, still bright with the glorious tints of October; and, through a deep ravine that divided them, a beautiful stream — rightly named "Roaring Brook" — came rushing down. On the other side from this, — that is, on the right, — Little Roaring Brook came leaping from the rocks in white cascades, and, disappearing for a moment under the railroad bridge, fell into the larger stream below. Then Lawrence had exciting glimpses of steaming colliery buildings, with their black mounds — almost mountains — of waste coal and slate from the mines, pushing out into the narrow valley. Then the train passed within sight of immense iron mills and blast furnaces flashing and flaming in the early twilight; then it came to a stop; and an omnibus whirled them away to a hotel in the city.

It was too late to see much of Scranton that night; but Lawrence consoled himself with anticipations of pleasure in going about with his uncle the next morning. He was, however, destined to be disappointed.

A tall gentleman, in gray overcoat and gray whiskers, whom he left talking with his uncle in the reading-room, was still at the hotel the next morning. After breakfast, a buggy came to the door of the hotel, — for himself and his uncle, Lawrence supposed; but no, it was for the tall gentleman; and the Doctor was going to ride with *him*.

"I've an engagement with this man," said the Doctor, taking his nephew aside; "and I see his buggy has seats for only two. But you won't mind being left alone for a few hours."

"O, certainly not," said Lawrence, with as cheerful a face as he could assume, though with a swelling heart. And his uncle rode away.

He watched the buggy as it disappeared up the long street; then a strange feeling of desolation came over him. The town was full of things worth seeing, but how could he, an utter stranger, hope to find them out? If he could only have gone in the buggy!

It was not his way, however, to spend much time in lamenting things that could not be helped. The morning was fine. The sunlight was beautiful on the mountains. "There's no use feeling bad," thought he. "I'm lucky to be here, any way. I can see the river and the city, if nothing else."

So he went out, in good spirits, and spent the forenoon very happily. Yet he was n't quite satisfied with himself when he returned to the hotel at dinner-time. He had seen and enjoyed many things, but not what he most wished to see, — the interior of a coal-mine. He had stood in silent wonder before more than one great colliery building, and heard the thundering crash of the coal dumped into the breakers; he had even looked into one, and seen the loaded cars from the deep mines whirled up swiftly, by the powerful engines, out of the black pit, and whirled back again empty, with terrible rapidity, and he had asked himself if he would ever have the courage to go down in one of them. He thought he would, if any one familiar with the mines would go with him; but everybody he saw appeared too busy to give a lad like him the least attention. "I must make acquaintances," thought he; and he determined to begin at the dinner-table, — his uncle not having returned.

At dinner, however, he was quite disheartened by what he saw. Sixteen young men sat at the same table with himself, and scarcely sixteen words were spoken by all of them during the solemn ceremony of eating. They were all good-looking, and had clean dickies, and white foreheads, and appeared so intelligent, and so much at their ease, that their unsocial behavior quite astonished him. Indeed, it overcame him so, that he would no more have ventured to break the awful silence by speaking loud than if he had been sitting in his uncle's church-pew during sermon-time.

II.

MR. CLARENCE AND HIS DOG MUFF.

WHILE he was wondering what they could all be thinking about, another young man entered, — a very young man, I may say, for his age could scarcely have exceeded that of Lawrence himself, although his surprisingly cool and self-possessed manners made him appear much older. He had a pleasant face, a jaunty short jacket, and large side-pockets. In these he carried his hands, and, in one of them, the end of a cane, which stuck up behind him at about the angle of a plough-handle. He looked around with a knowing expression, and finally, seeming, after mature thought on the subject, to have selected Lawrence as a table-companion, went and sat down opposite him.

"Here, Muff!" said he; and Lawrence noticed that he was followed by a very small dog, in a very large fleece of white curls, that made him look as if Nature had at first designed him for a dog, but had afterwards changed her mind, and finished him up as a sheep.

The young man took the cane from his pocket, held it up directly over the animal's upturned nose, and dropped it. Click! — the animal's jaws flew open like a trap, and caught it.

"Turn three times!" said the young man.

The animal immediately got up on his hind legs, with his head thrown back, balancing the stick, and began to revolve, like a capstan with a lever thrust through it.

"Go!" said the young man; and the dog, dropping down on all fours, still holding the cane, retired with it to the door of the dining-room, where he laid it down under the hat-table, and put his paws on it, and kept vigilant guard over it, against all comers. The tall head-waiter made one or two attempts to turn him out, but got growled and snapped at so smartly that he finally let him remain.

Everybody appeared to be amused by this trifling incident, especially some children at a table near by, who could not laugh enough to see the tall waiter retreat from such a tangled little ball of wool. Even the solemn young men relaxed their grave countenances, and from that moment became sociable.

Meanwhile, the dog's youthful master, not appearing in the least aware that either he or his pet had done anything extraordinary, glanced over the bill of fare, with the air of a person making judicious selections. Then he gave his order, calling the young lady who waited on him "Sis," and talking to her very much as if he had been an old friend of her father's and held her on his knee when she was little. Then, resting his arms on the table, he looked across it at Lawrence, and gave a short nod.

Lawrence gave a short nod in return.

"Fine day," said the young fellow.

"Beautiful," replied Lawrence, adding, "That 's a splendid pup of yours," — though he knew that *splendid* was n't just the word.

"He 'll do," said the young fellow, with a glance at the door. "'No dogs allowed in the dining-hall,' says the chap in the white apron, as I came in. 'Is that the rule of this hotel?' says I. 'Yes, sir,' says he. 'And a very good rule it is,' says I; 'but it don't say anything about sheep'; and, while we were talking, Muff and I walked in. I 'd like to see the place where Muff and I can't go! — Thank you, sis," to the young lady bringing his dinner. — "Acquainted in Scranton?"

Lawrence said no, — he arrived in town only the evening before with his uncle.

"Indeed! I came with *my* uncle, Mr. Fitz Adam, the celebrated mining engineer. You 've heard of him, of course?"

Lawrence was forced to own that he had not heard of the celebrated Mr. Fitz Adam. Thereupon the young fellow laid down his knife and fork, and looked at him over his plate with mild astonishment, making

Lawrence painfully aware how much he had lowered himself in his (the young fellow's) esteem by that confession.

"May I ask where you came from, sir?" he said, — as if that must be a curious country, indeed, where the inhabitants had never heard of his uncle.

Lawrence hardly knew at first what to make of this impertinence, but wisely concluded to make a joke of it.

"I am from Massachusetts," said he, with a droll smile just puckering the corners of his mouth. "And my uncle is the distinguished Doctor Dean. You have heard of him, of course?"

The young fellow laughed, and nodded at Lawrence approvingly; and Lawrence felt that this reply had raised him again in the young gentleman's esteem. "We are even on that. — Butter, if you please, sis. Thank you, sis. And see here, sis! — can't you get me a piping-hot sweet potato? I'll remember you in my will, if you'll be so kind as to oblige me." Then, turning again to Lawrence: "We're bound to speak well of our uncles, I see, though mine served me a remarkably shabby trick this morning."

"How so?"

"He left me asleep in my bed, and, as near as I can find out, went off to ride with another gentleman."

"Exactly what my uncle did by me!" said Lawrence, "only I was n't asleep in bed. Is your uncle a tall man in gray overcoat and gray whiskers?"

"The very same! You don't say he and your uncle — well! this is a coincidence! Your hand on it!" And the young fellow stretched his arm across the table. "My name," said he, "is Mr. Clarence Fitz Adam."

"Mine is Lawrence Livingstone." And from that moment they were friends.

"I wish you had been with me this morning," said Mr. Clarence, wiping his elbow, — for he had dipped it into the gravy when they shook hands. "I have seen Scranton outside, inside, and" — he pointed downward, mysteriously — "underside."

"Not in the coal-mines?" said Lawrence, with a pang of envy. "I wanted to go down in a shaft, but did n't know how the thing was to be done."

"You ain't bashful, I hope? You 'll find bashfulness don't pay, if you are going through the world," said Mr. Clarence, with an air of old experience. "The world 's a big shop. 'No admittance,' says the chap at the door. 'O, excuse me!' you say, and back out. But what do I say? 'No admittance? Certainly, that 's all right, — an excellent regulation; but, if you please, sir,' — then I go on and ask questions, and the first thing he knows, he is showing me round. Come, I 'll get my pup fed, then we 'll take a stroll together."

III.

SCRANTON AND COAL.

LAWRENCE was well pleased, for he was certain Mr. Clarence must be a capital fellow to go about with.

They walked down the street arm in arm, and crossed the river on the railroad bridge.

"This is the famous Lackawanna, as I suppose you have learned," said Mr. Clarence, pointing downwards at the hurrying water. "It is the stream that gives its name to all this coal region about Scranton. This side of the river," he continued, when they had crossed, "is Hyde Park. It is the fifth ward of the city. Let 's climb the bank above the railroad, and get a view. These," said he, turning, when they had reached a favorable point,—"these plain-looking little houses right before us here are miners' houses."

"I don't see but that they look very much like the houses of any other class of laborers," said Lawrence; "and I had imagined, somehow, they must be different,—little, low, black, dismal, mysterious huts, to correspond with the miners' dismal occupation, you know."

"They may be so in some countries. But in this favored land of liberty," said Mr. Clarence, smiling at his own eloquence, "the miners are so well paid, that they can afford to live very comfortably, as you see.

"Well," he went on, pointing with his cane, "there

MINERS' HOUSES, AND VIEW OF SCRANTON.

are the banks of the Lackawanna, and the railroad bridge we came over. We are here on the west bank; and there is the main part of the city on the east or left bank. This is all Scranton, — a fine, large city, as you see. But it has all been built up within a few years. A few years ago, this country was all a wilderness. Do you know what has made the difference? Coal, anthracite coal," Mr. Clarence continued, answering his own question. "Coal built those fine brick blocks, those churches, hotels, stores. Coal built those big blast furnaces and iron mills. Coal built the railroads you and I came in on yesterday. Coal has done all this, and more," — adding, by way of climax, "it has brought me the pleasure of your acquaintance."

"This is a funny-looking brick church, up on the hill behind us," said Lawrence, "with the end cracked open, and the sides held up with props."

"Yes. And just beyond it you'll see a house tipped up on one end, great pits in the earth, and other irregularities. Can you guess how they came about? Coal is to blame here too. There are mines all under where we stand. They extend like so many streets beneath the streets of the town, — two or three hundred feet below, of course. In place of houses and blocks down there, as you'll see, for we are going into a mine presently, they have what they call pillars, — pillars of coal, — which they leave to support the country above, when they are undermining it. That is a very important consideration, where a city stands. But it seems they did n't leave quite support enough under this part; for one day the ground began to shake and tremble; and it shook and trembled every little while, all that day and night, and all the next day, and the great pillars down there groaned and complained; and now and then the coal would fly off from them, as if it was angry, and the props — for they put wooden props under the roof besides — broke like pipe-stems; and finally, the next night, the crash came. The pillars had finally given way, and the country had settled. It looks now as if a young earthquake had kicked it."

"Who pays the damages under such circumstances?"

"I believe that question has n't been decided yet. The owner of the land sells house-lots, reserving the right to mine the coal under them. He sells the right to the coal companies. Coal companies take out too much coal, — crash, — down go the house-lots, with the houses on them. Who is to blame? You see, it is a delicate legal point," added Mr. Clarence, in his fine way. "And now, what do you say to going down and taking a look at that underground country?"

"I should be delighted to!" said Lawrence.

"Well, come along, I 've been here before, you see. Come, Muff!"

On their way they passed a little white box of a house, which Mr. Clarence said was the superintendent's office, and proposed that they should look in.

The interior consisted of one room, divided by a counter, on one side of which sat a young man reading a newspaper. Lawrence and Mr. Clarence, with the little dog Muff, advanced from the other side.

"Here," said Mr. Clarence, "is where the miners walk up and get their pay." He rapped on the counter with his cane. "How are you, Mr. Superintendent?"

The young man looked up pleasantly enough; and Mr. Clarence proceeded to introduce himself and his companion, with liberal allusions to their distinguished uncles, which made the more modest Lawrence grin and blush.

"We shall take it as a favor if you will grant us facilities for visiting the mines," said the fluent-tongued Mr. Clarence.

"It won't be safe for you to go into the mines without a guide, and I have no person to send with you," replied the superintendent, politely, but decidedly.

Upon which Lawrence was for retiring at once. But Mr. Clarence said, leaning upon the counter very much at his ease, "Of course; I understand all about that; and we have no wish to take up your valuable time. Thank you, — very kind, I am sure," — though Lawrence could n't see how the superintendent had shown himself so very kind, or why they should thank him. "Perhaps, however," said Mr. Clarence, "as my friend here is interested in the coal formation, you might show us some specimens without much trouble to yourself."

"O, certainly." The superintendent laid aside his newspaper, and got up from his chair. "Here is something quite pretty," said he, opening a drawer and placing on the counter a piece of slate-rock, bearing a beautiful impression of a fern-leaf. Lawrence's enthusiasm over it seemed to please him; and he continued to lay out his treasures, until he came to one which he pronounced "very remarkable."

This was a broad, thin slab of slate, which proved to be a perfect cast of a portion of the leaves of a strange tree, which must have been two or three feet in diameter, at least. All the minute seams in the bark, together with little bud-like spots occurring at regular intervals between parallel lines half an inch apart, were stamped with wonderful delicacy and distinctness in the slaty mould.

"How — where did these come from?" cried Lawrence, examining the specimens with astonishment and admiration.

"The coal, you know," said the voluble Mr. Clarence, "is supposed to be the result of immense, rank growths of fern-trees, and other plants, which absorbed the surplus carbon of the atmosphere during the carboniferous period. Carbon, you know, is the principal thing in coal, — the French say *charbon*, which means both carbon and coal, — and the carboniferous era is that in which our coal deposits were made. That was nobody knows how many thousands of years ago, — millions, it may be; and the trunks and leaves that made these impressions in the stones you are handling grew and decayed long before ever man appeared on the globe."

Lawrence knew as much as that before; but now, with the impressions before his eyes, distinct as if they had been taken but yesterday, the fact came home to his mind with startling force.

"Those forests," continued Mr. Clarence, "must have grown mostly in the water, and have sunk down in great beds of fallen trunks and matted leaves, and there decayed; and occasionally layers of mud or clay must have washed in over them; and now and then, at longer intervals,— the ground sinking, I suppose, — great beds of sand and pebbles washed in. The vegetable matters changed to coal, while the mud hardened into slate, and the sand and pebbles into rocks. The mud would often take impressions of the leaves and bark, and retain them, as it hardened, even after the leaves and bark themselves had changed to coal."

"See what you make of these," said the superintendent, smiling, as he handed out more specimens.

"These are fossil roots," said Mr. Clarence. "You find them generally in the fire clay under the coal veins; don't you? Ah, this," he said, seizing a beautiful slender, jointed stem of stone, — "this is a fossil reed! Something like it grows in Mexico, at this day."

"I believe you are right," said the superintendent. "That was fifteen feet long, when we first found it. But it has been broken, and I have given away pieces of it."

"Oh! if I could only have a piece!" exclaimed Lawrence.

"I'll give you a piece," said the superintendent, and picked out from the pile a small fragment of the reed, which had been previously broken off. Then, seeing how delighted the boy was, he selected a piece of slate that had a fine imprint of a leaf on it, and gave it to him.

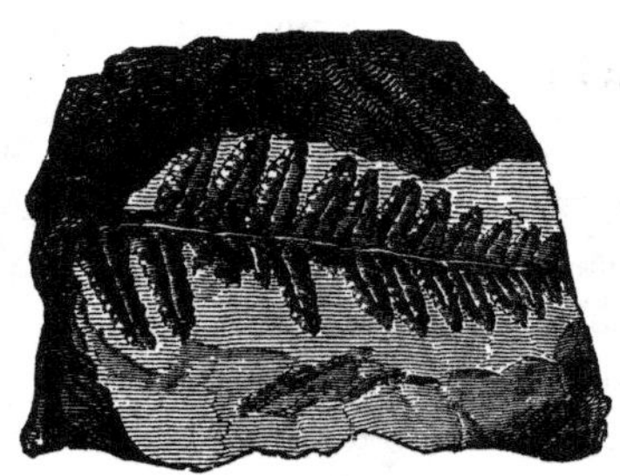

Lawrence, having secured these treasures, threw longing glances at the large cast already described. But of course the superintendent could not be expected to break that, for anybody. So Lawrence asked for a piece of paper, thinking he might take an impression from it.

"Now," said he, laying the paper on the cast, "if I only had a piece of lead to rub on it," — for he remembered that he had often, in this way, taken quite accurate impressions of cents and medals, when at school. "Have you a bullet?"

"None outside of me," said the superintendent; who went on to explain that he had one in him, received from a rebel musket.

"You were in the army, then?" said Mr. Clarence.

"Yes, with a company of our miners. We left coal, and went into business under the rebel fortifications. Our men helped make the famous mine we exploded before Petersburg. It was there I got my bullet."

As the said bullet was not available for artistic purposes, Lawrence tried a lead pencil, and succeeded in getting a fair impression of the curious bark pattern.

IV.

THE BREAKER.

"WOULD you like to look at the breaker?" then said the superintendent.

To which Lawrence replied, "O, very much!" while Mr. Clarence kicked his shin, and whispered, "That's the way to do it; I knew he would come round."

So they all walked out towards the great colliery building near by. It covered the steep slope of the hillside, and looked, Lawrence said, as if it might have been built as a coop for some long-necked, enormous bird.

"So it does," said the superintendent. "The highest part, which you fancy was meant to accommodate the goose's long neck and head, is what we call the tower. It is directly over the shaft. The wing covers, sloping away down to the railroad, are over the shoots."

"Spelled *chutes*," remarked Mr. Clarence, twisting his cane. "That is the French for falls. Did n't you ever hear a Frenchman speak of *la chute de Niagara?* You won't see a *chute de Niagara* here, but you'll see *chutes de* anthracite coal. Though in this case it is n't the cataracts they call the *chutes*, but the wooden spouts they run down."

The superintendent took them first into the engine-room, on the upper side of the building, close by the shaft. There they saw several beautiful engines at work with so little noise that they could scarcely be heard amid the thundering roar of the cataract of coal launched in the tower overhead.

"This engine is for pumping the water out of the mines," said the superintendent. "The one yonder works the ventilating fan, that blows out the impure air and smoke and fire-damp, and makes it possible for men to live so far down in the earth. Here is the breaker engine, that crushes the coal." Lastly, he showed a strong pair of engines employed in lifting the coal in the shaft.

"You don't have to go far for the fuel you burn," said Lawrence, as they went on into the boiler-room.

"Show him," said the superintendent to a stout fireman, who threw open the iron doors beneath the boilers, and exposed to view a glowing and flaming bed of the very finest kind of coal, "no bigger than peas," Lawrence said.

"We call it pea-coal," replied the superintendent. "It is too fine to ship, and we used to throw it away with the coal-dust. But since coal has been so high, we have tried burning it here, and find that it does very well."

Returning through the engine-room, they entered the tower, and stopped at the head of the shaft. This had for Lawrence a terrible fascination. Every three quarters of a minute — as Mr. Clarence, who looked at his watch, informed them — up came out of its black depths, with fearful rapidity, a car-load of coal, shooting past them, and disappearing with a deafening crash in the top of the tower, high above their heads.

The shaft was double, and two sets of cars were ascending and descending, with a parting of timber between them. The car was supported on a strong framework, called a carriage, which was lifted and lowered by a long rope and a steam-engine.

"What if the rope should break?" said Lawrence, imagining the frightful consequences of such a disaster.

"Don't you see?" said Mr. Clarence, pointing with his cane; "the carriage runs in the grooves of these upright timbers. They are called guides. You see the notches in them. Well, if the rope breaks, there are dogs — as we call them — in the sides of the carriage, and they fall into the notches, and hold it."

"I see you know something about coal," remarked the superintendent.

"I ought to," replied Mr. Clarence. "I intend to follow my uncle's profession"; and he took occasion once more to extol that celebrated mining engineer. "It is one of the noblest professions in the world. Civil engineering is nothing to it. A civil engineer, laying out a railroad, or anything of the sort, works where he can see; but a mining engineer has to work like a mole in the dark. He must know all about the coal-beds, how they lie, and the easiest and most economical way of getting at them, and all that. Now when you consider that the coal-beds in these anthracite regions lie in all sorts of ways, — as if the country, after they were formed, had been tossed up like the waves of a sea by the action of heat, I suppose; so that here you find them nearly level, in a sort of basin, and there turned up edgeways, and in another place, perhaps, regularly rolled over and folded together, like that," — he traced out with his cane, on the floor, the various undulations and curves in the coal strata, very much as if he had been writing a hard word; "when you consider all that, and reflect that sometimes these beds crop out at the surface, and sometimes dive hundreds of feet into the earth, — you 'll conclude that a mining engineer, who knows his business, knows something."

"There are plenty who pretend to know their business who don't know the first thing about it," said the superintendent.

"Yes, and they often come and get my uncle to go and engineer for them," said Mr. Clarence. "'But you are an engineer, yourself,' says my uncle. 'Yes, but my eyes trouble me, — I can't see very well,' says the fellow. So my uncle goes and gives him a start, and makes figures and plans for him to work after. O," laughed Mr. Clarence, "lots of those fellows have poor eyes, when anything requiring real skill is to be done; though they pass for engineers and draw big salaries. They know just enough to open a drift, or a slope, when it has been laid out for them."

"What is a *drift*, or a *slope?*" Lawrence asked.

"Why, you see, there are different ways of opening a coal-mine. One is by a *shaft*, like this, when the beds lie deep, and in a sort of basin. We go straight down to the bottom of the lowest bed we are going to work, and pump out the water and draw up the coal by steam. The *drift* is a gangway from the bottom of the shaft, or a straight opening into a nearly level coal-bed, where it crops out on some hillside; and there the engineer must be pretty sharp, in order to make his opening so that the mine will drain itself, and the coal can be drawn out by mules. The *slope* is an opening that goes down slantingly into a vein; in it a track is laid, and regular wheel-cars are let down and drawn up by a steam-engine."

Lawrence wished to know more about the shaft before them; and the superintendent explained that it was a perpendicular opening, twenty-two feet long, twelve broad, and two hundred and fifty feet deep. It had been sunk by drilling and blasting through the solid strata of rock that covered and separated the coal-beds. It was divided, by partitions of plank and timber, into what seemed three separate shafts, — two for the coal-carriages, and a third for the air column and water-pump, which ventilated and drained the mines.

"But what is the use of a high tower?" said Lawrence, his eyes following a coal-car as it shot up amid the strong timbers and braces above his head.

"To get room to break, screen, and separate the

coal," said the superintendent. "Come up stairs, and you will see."

The tower was fifty feet high above the mouth of the shaft; and it would have had to be built still higher, Mr. Clarence observed, had not the slope of the hill made room for the bins below. They went up by narrow wooden staircases, through the "screen-room" and "plate-room" (which the superintendent said they should see again as they came down), amidst clouds of coal-dust, and blackened beams and braces, to the summit of the black-raftered and high-windowed tower. Mr. Clarence came last, having stopped to set Muff to guarding his cane in the engine-room, in order to prevent that white sheep of a dog from becoming a black one.

"Here you'll see what makes the noise," said the superintendent.

As he spoke, up came a coal-car, and stopped before their eyes. It was loaded, as Lawrence now had a chance to see, with huge lumps or fragments, some of immense size and weight. It seemed endowed with intelligence of its own, for the moment it arrived in the right place it threw out its own end-board, and immediately tipped up, casting its contents into an opening through the floor, called a "dump." Some of the great lumps tumbled over the sides of the opening, and made Lawrence jump to take care of his toes.

An attendant ("That's the ticket-boss," said Mr. Clarence), begrimed from head to foot with coal-dust, now stepped forward, tumbled the scattered lumps into the dump, took something from a little hook in the car, pulled a bell as a signal to the engineer, and closed up the end-board as the empty car fell back into its place on the carriage. The car now dropped swiftly down into the shaft again; while the man, glancing at the little thing he had taken out of it, proceeded to put it away in a box of pigeon-holes.

"That 's the ticket," said Mr. Clarence. "You did n't know they had to have tickets on these cars, did you?"

Lawrence looked puzzled, and the superintendent explained. "This little piece of brass"—he took the ticket from its pigeon-hole—"has a number on it. It is number thirty-seven. That is the number of the chamber or breast in which that load of coal was mined. There is one miner in each chamber; he has his package of tickets, and he puts one in every car he sends out. The tickets are collected by the ticket-boss here, and all the thirty-sevens are put into pigeon-hole thirty-seven. So with the other tickets. Then, at night, the tickets in each pigeon-hole show just how many loads of coal are to be credited to each miner."

"How many, on an average, will there be?"

"Seven is the rule; and each car-load must be a ton and a half."

"Do you weigh it?"

"No. The ticket-boss can tell by his eye if it is full weight. If it is n't, he docks the miner for the deficiency. Or he docks him if there is too much slate in his coal."

"Seven car-loads, — a ton and a half to the load, — ten and a half tons," said Lawrence. "Does one miner get out all that, in a day?"

"You must know there are two distinct classes of laborers in the mines," said the superintendent. "Each miner has possession of a chamber and we deal only with him. He finds his own tools, powder, oil, everything; and hires a common laborer to help him. The laborer knows not much more about mining than you do, and he is not called a miner, though he works in the mines. He loads the coal, and helps the miner in many ways. These two get out their seven loads, — or more, if they choose; and we pay the miner ninety-seven cents a load."

"Six dollars and seventy-nine cents a day!" said Lawrence, who was quick at figures. "That's good wages."

"So it is, even after the miner has paid his expenses out of it. His powder costs him a dollar a day. He pays his laborer now, I believe, two dollars and ten cents a day. He has nearly three dollars and a half left for himself, even if he gets out only seven loads. But some miners get out eight or nine loads a day; and, after making due allowance for stoppages, on account of accidents, or a dull market, earn their thousand or twelve hundred dollars a year. You will notice that those who confine themselves to their seven loads will go home this afternoon at three or four o'clock."

"What sort of people are they?" Lawrence wished to know.

"They are all Welsh, in these mines. And a respectable, thrifty class they are, generally. They have their church-meetings, and their Sunday school, and week-day school for their children, like any other class. A few of them are dissipated and shiftless, and spend all they earn. But the most of them are sober and industrious, and provide well for their families. Some have laid up handsome little fortunes, all earned in the mines."

"They are a much better class than the miners down in the Schuylkill district," said Mr. Clarence. "There we have all sorts, but mostly Irish of the worst kind. Every once in a while some of them will get up a strike. The strikers go round to all the mines, and force everybody to stop work until everybody gets an increase of wages. If they don't like a boss, they give him warning to quit, and if he don't quit they kill him. Riots are quite common, and the governor has had to call out the militia to put them down."

"How many miners are at work in this mine?" Lawrence asked. "And how many men, besides?"

"We have forty-eight chambers running now; that makes forty-eight miners," said the superintendent. "These, with their laborers, and a small army of men and boys employed in various other ways, — mule drivers, slate-pickers, and so forth, — make a force of over three hundred."

All the while they were talking the loads of coal kept thundering into the dump. They now descended into the room below, to see what next became of it. There it was received on a set of strong, slanting iron plates, forming a sort of spout from the dump above to the breaker below, and so arranged as to let the small pieces of coal drop through between them, as the cataract poured down. The big lumps rushed on to the breaker, guided by four stout Irishmen, armed with strong iron rakes. There was something terrible in the way the great lumps and blocks of anthracite came crashing and bounding down these plates; and Lawrence observed that the men had to work hard to take care of them.

"Yes," one said; "the coal bosses us. If we had a boss that drove us half as hard, we'd be kickin' him out." And he grinned through his grime of coal-dust.

The breaker looked like a great coffee-mill; and the most of the coal went into its hopper. To see what became of it after it was crushed, the lads followed their guide to the room below.

Here was a lively scene. The first thing Lawrence noticed was a long, cylindrical screen, as large as a good-sized saw-log, rolling over and over, high up in the back part of the room. It was sifting the crushed coal, which was poured into one end of it by a spout from the breaker above. It was inclined just enough to let the coal roll and rattle down slowly from the upper towards the lower end, as it revolved. The

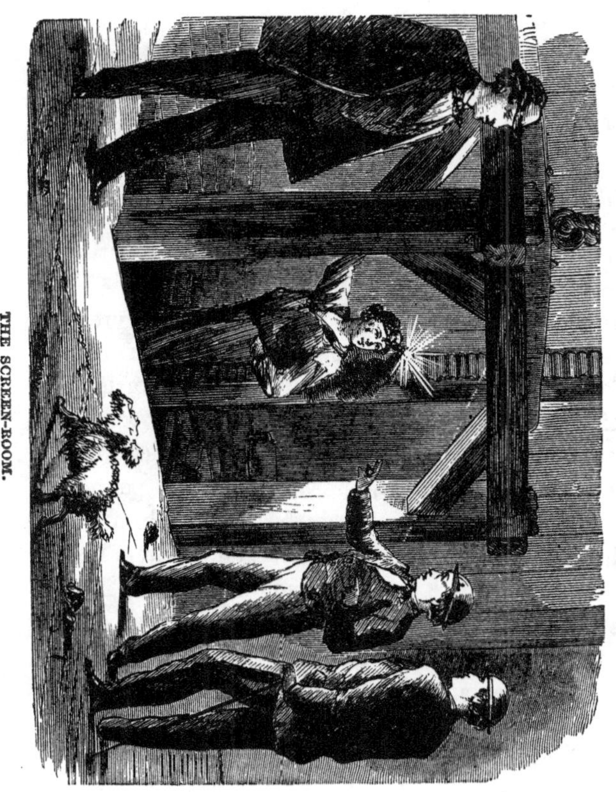

THE SCREEN-ROOM.

finest coal and dust fell out of it, first, into a second screen, which separated them. Next, coal of four different sizes fell into four separate spouts, or chutes, the largest size coming out of the coarsest meshes at the lower end of the screen. These screens and chutes occupied one entire division of the room; and Lawrence now saw that there was another division, the exact counterpart of this; so that there were in all four screens and eight chutes. The two upper screens slanted each way from the breaker above, and the chutes distributed the torrent of coal into little streams which poured down through the room.

Here were the "pickers"; and quick-fingered, sharp-eyed, black-nosed little people they were. There were over forty in the room, — boys of various ages, sitting on the sides of the chutes, or on boards laid across, one above the other, picking out pieces of slate and "bony" coal, as the black streams poured down. What one did not get, those below him on the chute were expected to see and take out. The little hands flew fast; and the bad pieces went into wooden "slate-pockets" between the chutes. Lawrence, who could scarcely tell slate from coal at first sight, was amazed at their quickness of eye and hand.

"They are certainly throwing away coal!" said he, taking a lump which one was casting out.

"That's nothing but bone," said Mr. Clarence. "It came very near being coal, but I suppose there was a little too much earthy mud mixed with the carbon of the decaying forests. All our coal-beds are full of slaty and bony seams, as you will see when we go into the mines."

"The best we can do," said the superintendent, "a good deal of slate comes to the breaker, and has to be picked out here. The miners call it *collum*. *Culm* is the proper word. They call everything *collum* that goes into the waste heap. Would you like to look at that?"

They went down into an archway beneath the screen-room, where they found a mule-car loading under a spout which led from one of the culm-bins. The car filled, the spout was closed, and the mule was driven off with his load along a track laid across the summit of an immense black mound, or small mountain, as it might truly be called. It spread out into the valley below, and must have contained hundreds of thousands of tons of "collum,"—being composed entirely of slate and bone and coal-dust from this single colliery.

"We dump here a hundred and twenty-five loads a day," said the superintendent.

"In and about Scranton," remarked Mr. Clarence, "there are a dozen collieries, and each one has just such a 'collum dump,' as they call it. You have only to go around and look at them, to get a tolerably big idea of the coal business of this little town."

On the steep sides of the black mountain three or four women and one crippled old man were picking out the best pieces of bony coal, or pieces of slate to

6*

which a little coal adhered, and putting them into bags and baskets to burn or to sell.

From the culm dump the superintendent took his young friends down the hill-slope to the coal-bins, under the chutes, and showed them a coal-train loading from spouts.

"So you don't have to shovel or handle the coal at all," said Lawrence.

"Not from the time it leaves the miner's chamber. From there it is drawn by mules to the foot of the shaft; then it is lifted by machinery, and poured through the breaker and down the chutes, travelling by its own weight, until it is taken off by the cars here. Even the cars, as you see," added the superintendent, "are so constructed that the coal can be dumped from them on to a coal-wharf, or into the hold of a vessel, through spouts, still without handling."

V.

THE SHAFT.

They now returned to the engine-room, where Mr. Clarence found Muff keeping faithful guard over his cane. "Present arms!" said Mr. Clarence. And Muff, getting up on his hind legs and turning about, with the cane balanced in his mouth, allowed his master to take it out. "Thank you," said Mr. Clarence. And after that the dog went wherever the boys did.

"I see you looking anxiously at the shaft," said the superintendent, smiling at Lawrence. "Won't you be afraid to go down?"

"I don't think I shall be afraid to go where anybody else does," said Lawrence, gazing down into the shaft. But even as he spoke, he started back.

Suddenly up out of the black pit rose a figure like a ghost. It was a moment before Lawrence perceived that it was really a form of flesh and blood, and, moreover, a boy of about his own age. He was standing on the naked beams of the carriage, with just one hand outstretched, holding on by a brace. This was all that supported him on his dark journey up the shaft. There was a little tin lamp hooked into his cap, the sallow flame of which, together with spots and streaks of coal-dust on his face, gave a sort of unearthly cast to his complexion. He wore no coat, and his shirt was open at the throat. The carriage stopped when on a level with the floor at the head of the shaft; he stepped off, and it sank down into the pit again.

"How would you like to ride in that style?" asked the superintendent.

Lawrence thought that if another boy could hold on he could, and said he would like it.

"Well," said the superintendent, "I think we can do a little better by you than that. These boys ride up and down any way. I shall expect to see them clinging on to the rope like monkeys, soon. Owen," said he to the ghost, "I want you to go through the

THE COAL-SHAFT.

mines with these young gentlemen, if you have time."

"I 've time enough," said Owen; and his face lighted up with a bright and friendly smile, — not at all ghostly.

"What did I tell you?" Mr. Clarence whispered to Lawrence, while the superintendent went for another lamp.

The lamp was brought, — a little teapot-shaped thing, with a hook for a handle, and a lighted wick in the spout. Lawrence took it. Then an empty car was stopped at the head of the shaft, and the three lads stepped into it, — Mr. Clarence with Muff in his arms. Then the signal was given; the car began to sink; and darkness surrounded them, streaked only by the dim rays of the lamps.

"Good by," cried the superintendent, from above.

"Good by," echoed the voices of the boys, from the depths of the hollow-sounding shaft.

Down, down went the car, steadily, but by no means so fast as when it bore no freight of human lives. Lawrence held tight to his little lamp with one hand, and to the brace with the other, while he tried to get some idea of the depth of the shaft, by reflecting that, if the partitions were taken out, Bunker Hill Monument would have made a very good plug for it.

"Are you afraid?" said Owen, laughing. "A terrible accident happened in a shaft near here the other day"; and a shadow passed over his face at the recollection. "A crowd of men were going into the mines one morning. They did n't like to wait, so seventeen of 'em piled on to one car at once. The rope broke, and they fell two hundred feet. Fourteen got killed, and the other three got maimed for life."

"That 's a cheerful story to tell, when we are halfway down a shaft," said Mr. Clarence.

"I thought you said there were iron dogs to fall into these notches in the guides, and hold the car, if the rope should break," said Lawrence.

"The dogs would hold a loaded car that was going up, or a light load going down," said Owen.

"Because," added Mr. Clarence, "a car going up must stop before it can fall; but, going down, it is already in motion, and if it has a heavy load on, it will break everything before it. But here we are, all right. Step out."

Lawrence was at first so bewildered that he hardly knew which way to step. He seemed to have dropped suddenly into the heart of an immense, black, branching cavern. Strange noises filled his ears, and glancing lights moved like fireflies through the darkness. Then dim forms and sooty faces and shining eyes appeared around him. Everything had such an unearthly look, that for a moment he could have fancied that he was in the bottomless pit, and that these were its proper inhabitants.

"Lean on me, look!" said Owen, "then you shall not black yourself." So Lawrence got out of the car without rubbing his clothes against it. "This way, look!" cried Owen, again. "There 's water!"

The reservoir, or well, from which the water of the mines was pumped, was directly beneath the car, at the foot of the shaft; and Lawrence thought he meant that. In avoiding it he ran under a little streaming shower that dripped from some point above — which was, in fact, the water Owen had wished to warn him against.

"What a stupid fellow I am!" he exclaimed. "There goes my light!" — his little teapot of a lamp having been extinguished in his brief passage under the shower-bath.

"Never mind; I can light it," said Owen; and whilst he was touching the flame of his own to the drenched wick, Lawrence had time to look about him and see more plainly where they were.

He now perceived that the lights and the demons he had seen were men and boys with lamps on their caps, and that the sounds he heard were the shouts of mule-drivers and the tinkling of mule-bells, mingled with the noise of water falling into the well.

"Now you see where the loads of coal come from," said Mr. Clarence.

The empty car in which they made the descent had already been pushed off from the carriage, along a track laid level with it; and now a loaded car, standing near by, was seized by men and boys, and pushed on. A bell-wire was then pulled ("Signal for the engineer," said Mr. Clarence), and up went the carriage, with the car on it, disappearing instantly in the darkness of the shaft.

"Hark!" said Mr. Clarence. And in a few seconds they heard the faint thunder-peal of a load of coal dumped into the breaker three hundred feet above.

"That 's disposing of a ton and a half of coal on short notice," said Mr. Clarence. And almost while he was speaking the car came down again empty.

Then another car was pushed on, and sent up. There was a long row of loaded cars waiting on the track, and others were coming in little trains of four or five, drawn by mules, out of the depths of the cavern. The whole made a picture which, seen by the dim light of the lamps, in the midst of surrounding blackness, had a strange fascination for the eyes of Lawrence.

Mr. Clarence now put down his dog Muff, and told him to take care of himself.

"I should think he would get as dirty here as in the breaker," said Lawrence.

"It 's a different kind of dirt," said Mr. Clarence. "It will be all on the outside, if he rubs against anything. But in the breaker he would get the coal-dust sifted into his wool, so it could never be washed out."

"See here a minute," said Owen; and he led Lawrence to a frame of rough boards, like a box, set into the wall of the cavern. There were two holes in it, like a pair of great eyes, and he told Lawrence to look in through one of them.

Lawrence climbed up on a ledge of slate, put his eye to the hole, and uttered an exclamation of surprise. He had expected to see nothing but darkness, in such a place; but it was like looking into a show-box.

"What do you see?" said Mr. Clarence.

"I see a little room, with a clock in it."

"What time is it?" asked Owen.

"Ten minutes past three, — as plain as can be! Where does the light come from on the face of the clock?"

Lawrence looked around, and saw Owen at his side laughing.

"Where *did* it come from? Look again," said Owen.

He looked again, and declared that the box was as dark as a pocket. Then in an instant it was lighted up again. Turning his head quickly, he saw Owen holding a lamp at the other hole.

"Why do you keep a clock boxed up in that way?" he asked.

"It 's handy, look!" said Owen. "A man wants to know the time; he puts his eye to one hole, and his lamp to the other, and there it is. If the clock was n't boxed up, it would n't be there to-morrow."

"I see," said Lawrence, who understood that it would be stolen.

A number of men, with lamps on their hats and tin pails in their hands, were coming along by the railroad track, and crowding near the shaft.

"They have got through work, and are waiting to go up," said Owen.

Half a dozen of them jumped into the next empty car that came down, the engineer was signalled to lift slowly, and up they went to the head of the shaft.

VI.

IN THE GANGWAY.

"I SEE here but one set of cars going up and down," said Lawrence. "But at the head of the shaft they were moving on both sides."

"We are working two veins of coal," said Owen. "This is what we call the Rock Vein; the other is the Diamond Vein, thirty feet above. The other cars stop there."

"Thirty feet! and what is between the two veins?"

"Slate, mostly. There 's always layers of sandstone, limestone, slate, clay, — one or all of 'em, — between the different coal veins," said Owen. And seeing the astonishment of Lawrence, who, after all he had heard and read on the subject, had but a faint idea of a coal formation, he continued, "Fifty feet below this vein there is another, — what we call the Big Vein, — fourteen feet thick. Then there are five more veins below that. There are two more above the Diamond. They will all pay to work, some day, after we get these two veins worked out. Then there are several little veins besides."

"By *veins*," said Mr. Clarence, "he means *seams* or *beds*. Coal lies in layers, which can't properly be called *veins*, though this is the term used everywhere in the anthracite regions, — except by my uncle and myself," he added, with pleasing vanity. "Some minerals lie in *streaks;* and those are properly called *veins.* Go into the soft-coal regions, and you won't hear coal-beds called *veins.*"

"Why are they called so here?"

"I suppose it is because the anthracite beds are so tumbled and broken up in some places. Just here you see them lying nearly all on a level, or undulating something like the surface of a hilly country. But go into mines where I have been! Some of the seams are perpendicular, or keeled over, or broken up by faults, so that it appears ridiculous to call them beds."

"Are n't the soft-coal beds tumbled up too?"

"Nothing like the anthracite. They all lie as nearly level as these beds here. There 's a very pretty scientific fact connected with this difference in the two formations," Mr. Clarence continued. "Soft coal is more or less bituminous, while anthracite has no bitumen in it. But there 's no doubt but what they were both formed in the same way, and out of the same materials. The ancient forests I told you of decayed in the water and made black mud, which a certain degree of heat and pressure condensed into soft coal. There the bituminous coal-fields were left, and were not much disturbed afterwards. But in the anthracite region there was subsequent volcanic action, which heaved and broke up the coal measures, and with its intense heat expelled the bituminous matters and hardened the coal still more. The best evidence in support of this theory is, that here you have igneous rocks, — or rocks that were melted matter when they were heaved up from the bowels of the earth, — while in the bituminous regions you have none."

"Are the anthracite regions as extensive as the bituminous?"

"My dear sir, nothing in comparison. The biggest part of the anthracite coal-field lies in Luzerne and Schuylkill Counties, here in Eastern Pennsylvania; while the bituminous coal-fields extend over nearly all the western portion of the State, and over large portions of other States, and over other parts of the world; though I believe," added Mr. Clarence, "that a little anthracite is found, in the neighborhood of igneous rocks, in some bituminous regions. This is all Greek to you, is n't it, my little Welshman?" he said to Owen.

"I don't understand anything about it," replied Owen, laughing.

"I knew it," said Mr. Clarence. "It is singular, — men who work in coal-mines all their lives generally know nothing more about the history of the coal formation than your day-laborers in Massachusetts. Some men who call themselves mining engineers are just as ignorant. Yet this Welsh boy can tell you all about the coal, as it lies in the mines, and the gangways and chambers are as familiar to him as the streets of your native village are to you. How thick, Owen, is this 'Rock Vein,' as you call it?"

"Nine feet," replied Owen, quickly. "The Diamond Vein is seven feet."

"All solid coal?" said Lawrence, looking at the black wall of the cavern.

"All but the slate in it. The coal is in three benches," said Owen.

Then Lawrence had to ask what benches were; and Mr. Clarence was well pleased to be able to inform him.

"I told you how layers of slate occur in the coal-beds, did n't I? The bed may be even twenty or thirty feet thick, but it won't be one clean body of coal. Every two or three feet, or oftener, you come to a thin seam of slate running through it. The coal that lies in these natural divisions, between the slate seams, we call benches. Here there is a roof of slate." Mr. Clarence took the lamp from Lawrence's hand, and held it high above their heads. "Then, between that and the bottom," — passing the lamp down the wall, — "there are two slate seams; see if you can tell where they are."

"It all looks alike to me, coal and slate," said Lawrence, his eye glancing along the uniform blackness of the wall. "Ah!" he suddenly exclaimed, "I see! This little ridge! Here must be one of the slate seams! and here is the other!"

"You would make a miner," said Owen, smiling, as they walked on.

"Are *you* a miner?" Lawrence asked.

"My father is, and I mean to be. I come down at noon to bring his dinner, and stop and help him sometimes."

"Do you like it?"

"I like it well. If you work in the mines awhile," said Owen, "you never want to do anything else. Once a miner, always a miner,' my father says."

"Why so?" said Lawrence.

"The miner is his own boss, look," said Owen, stopping, and facing the visitors, his bright Welsh eyes shining with animation under his lamp-hung cap. "He can work, or he can sit still. He works six or eight hours a day, and earns good pay. It is never hot and it is never cold in the mines. It is about the same thing the year round. You work here a few years; then you go to work outside, and it is bad. You can't stand the heat. You can't stand the cold. You are glad to get back into the mines."

They walked on again, keeping the car-track, between black walls of coal. "It is like a street railroad," said Lawrence, — "only the track is narrow, and the street is n't so wide as I thought it was."

"This is what we call a gangway, or drift," said Mr. Clarence. "It is the main passage from the breasts or chambers to the shaft. It is cut out just the depth of the coal-bed, and wide enough to accommodate the cars. In thin coal-beds, — they often work those that are only two or three feet thick, — they cut down enough of the top rock to make a passage for the cars.

"And to give the miners room to work, I suppose," said Lawrence.

"No," said Owen; "miners can work where a man

can't stand. My father once worked in a coal-vein, in the old country, where he had to lie on his side when he used the pick. The vein was only a foot and a half thick; but he got out the coal."

"Then why not invent a low car, that will carry the coal through low gangways, and save cutting out the rock?" said Lawrence.

"To invent a low car is easy enough," said Mr. Clarence, with a laugh at his friend's simplicity; "but it is n't so easy to invent a low mule."

Owen laughed too. Lawrence was glad his blushes were hidden by the darkness of the drift. But, to show that he had not spoken so inconsiderately as Mr. Clarence supposed, he retorted quickly, "Haul the cars by machinery; — why not?"

"That 's not so bad an idea," said Mr. Clarence, his respect for his friend's intelligence somewhat restored.

"My father tells how, in the old country, women used to carry the coal out of the mines," said Owen. "The men mined it, and the women carried it. A woman would carry a load of coal heavier than she was up slopes, or stairs; and maybe she would have a quarter of a mile to travel before she could put it down."

"That is a horrible story!" said Lawrence, who had never seen women do hard work, and could scarcely believe that such things were tolerated in a Christian country.

"A reform, in this respect, has taken place in the British collieries, within a few years," said Mr. Clarence. "Now a small steam-engine that burns only four or five tons of coal a day does work it would take five hundred women to do."

Lawrence concluded that steam was a good missionary, if it could convert people from such barbarous practices.

"It is the great agent of modern civilization," said Mr. Clarence, in his eloquent way. "Our steamships, railroads, factories, a thousand industrial enterprises, are dependent upon it; but what is steam itself dependent on? Without coal, steam would be a limping cripple. This big black fellow, in whose bed we now are, is doing a good share of the work of the world. Did I say four or five tons did the work of five hundred women? It is a low estimate. Ten pounds of coal, economically applied to steam-power, are considered equal to a day's work by one man. Then a ton and a half of coal may be set down as equal to the labor of one man for a year. I have seen a careful calculation, to that effect, in one of my uncle's books."

"I wonder who first thought of digging out coal and burning it," said Lawrence.

"Nobody knows who first used soft coal for fuel," Mr. Clarence replied. "It has been in use in England for hundreds of years, though it was only after the forests began to disappear, and the steam-engine was invented, and gas-light came into fashion, that the immense coal-trade was developed which now makes the prosperity of that little island. This anthracite business is another thing. It has all been developed within fifty years, though there is evidence that the first blacksmiths in the country began to use the stone coal, as it was called (*anthracite* is only a Greek word for the same thing), a hundred years ago. It took the rest of the world half a century to find out how to burn the thing. Neither philosophers nor fools could make a fire of it, in a common stove or fire-place. Bituminous coal will kindle and burn with a flame like wood; but hard coal required different treatment, and a peculiar kind of grate. Then, when it did burn, it was found superior to any other coal for many purposes. Though hard to kindle, it makes an intense heat, and no smoke. And now," Mr. Clarence concluded, "though it is confined to so small an area, compared with the vast fields of bituminous coal, there is about as much anthracite mined in this State, every year, as there is of other coal."

Meanwhile, the boys walked on through the black gangway, which seemed interminable to Lawrence. It was lighted only by the two little lamps they carried, which made a dim halo about them, in the midst of darkness that retreated slowly before, and followed close behind, as they moved on. Occasionally, little incidents diversified the gloomy monotony of the trip. Now they approached a faintly-shining beam, seen afar off in the cavernous darkness, which grew to a little yellow glow in a corner, as they came near, and proved to be the light of a tiny lamp on the ground, close under the wall of coal. Sitting near it, between

THE DOORKEEPER.

two stout wooden props supporting the slate roof, was a boy, who seemed at first glance a mere imp of darkness. He was not more than nine or ten years old, and O so small and black! He seemed to be playing with something on a black slab of slate, between him and the lamp. On coming up to him, what was Lawrence's surprise to see that the little fellow was amusing himself, there in the solitude of the mine, with a pack of cards almost as black as his fingers.

Close by was a large wooden door which completely closed the gangway, — " to shut off the air-current, and force it in another direction," Mr. Clarence said, — and this child was the doorkeeper.

" Are n't you lonesome here ? " Lawrence asked.

" Not much," the urchin replied, looking up with a grin. " It ain't so nice when my lamp burns out, and I can't get oil. But the mule-teams are passing all the time."

While he was speaking the shout of a driver was heard, and a light was seen approaching. Then appeared a train of empty cars, accompanied by a boy, with the usual lamp on his hat. The child sprang to his feet, and threw the gate open ; Owen and the two visitors stepped aside between the props of the gangway ; the train passed through, the driver shouting to the trampling mules, and the great door flapped together again.

The visitors and their guide soon followed the train, while the little fellow returned to his cheerful game of cards.

" How I pity him !" said Lawrence. " I wish I could give him something to amuse him, alone there in the dark ! "

" He is well enough off," laughed Owen. " He is happy. You should hear my father tell of boys in the mines of the old country, who can't even have a light."

Along a channel beside the gangway flowed a rivulet

towards the shaft, — its low, gentle ripple sounding hollow and strange in those dismal depths. That was all the noise they heard for some distance, as they walked on. Then suddenly came a terrific thunder-peal, which seemed to shake the earth, and made Lawrence for a moment think the roof was coming down upon their heads.

"Now here we are, look!" was all the comment Owen made upon this little incident, which might well startle a stranger.

VII.

THE MINERS AT WORK.

THEY passed a railroad switch, and followed a side track, which turned off into what seemed a winding cavern. It was narrow at the entrance, but it grew wider and wider, as they advanced. All was dark before them at first, but as they kept on around the curve of the track, dim lights appeared, glimmering through a thick, bluish cloud. The broad, flat roof was supported by rows of wooden props. Beside the car-track were heaps of slate that had been taken out of the coal. And now Lawrence, if he had not already guessed the nature of the explosion he had heard, was made aware of it by the strong odor of blasting-powder which swept over him with a cloud of smoke.

"This is what we call a chamber, or breast," said Mr. Clarence.

At the farther end of it, where the lights were, seventy-five or eighty yards from the entrance, two men were at work in the thickest of the smoke. One was clearing away the fragments which the blast had blown out from the bottom of the coal-seam. This was the miner's "laborer." The other was examining the opening that had just been made, and evidently studying how to place his next charge of powder. This was the miner himself. Both were begrimed with powder-smoke and coal-dust, the effect of which was heightened, to Lawrence's imagination, by the cloud and stench in which they worked.

Owen stepped nimbly over the rubbish, the others following, — all but Muff. Mr. Clarence had left him, with his cane, at the entrance to the chamber. Then Owen astonished Lawrence very much by saying quietly, as the miner turned and looked at them, with an honest, kindly face under its grime, —

"This is my father."

Lawrence was, in fact, taken so much by surprise at this introduction, that he offered to shake hands, — an evidence of weakness on his part that once more, for the moment, quite lost him the respect of his friend, Mr. Clarence.

The sensible Welshman declined the honor, showing his blackened hands, and said, "You have come to see the coal-mines, have you?"

Lawrence said he had, and began to ask questions with regard to the manner in which the coal was got out.

THE COAL-MINER.

"It is very simple, look!" replied the miner. (The father, like the son, had an odd way of throwing in that little word *look*, when he was speaking.) "You put in your charge of powder, and blow it out."

"Do you have to blow all of it?"

"Every yard. I work under the vein, look. I work out here a space, at the bottom, about five feet high, and twelve feet deep. Then I put in a heavy charge above, and blow down the top."

"How much coal do you blow out at a time?"

"A couple of tons or so, when I am working out the bottom. Then when I blow down the top, I get a good many tons, sometimes."

"You must drill pretty deep for that."

"Yes, we sink the drill five or six feet generally, to get a good blast. There 's everything in taking advantage of the way the coal lays. It is n't like mining soft coal, look. There you work under the bottom bench with a pick, and then break down the rest from the top with wedges. You don't blast at all, only when the rock is in your way."

"What sound is that?" asked Lawrence.

Both men had stopped work for the moment; and now could be heard a regular, dull *click-click-click*, which seemed to be somewhere in the solid wall of coal close beside them.

"That is the miner drilling in the next chamber."

"How far off is he?"

"About twenty feet. He keeps his breast along about even with mine. We are in, now, about two hundred and fifty feet from the gangway."

"How deep do you drive your chambers?"

"About three hundred feet, along here. Sometimes we go deeper, and sometimes not so deep."

"Then how do you get out the coal beyond?"

"Drive breasts from other gangways," said the miner.

Lawrence could have remained a long time watching him at his work, and talking with him; but Owen suggested that they had a great deal yet to see, and that it was getting late. So they took leave of the miner, and started to go back to the entrance to the chamber, where Mr. Clarence had left Muff.

In the next chamber they found two men and a boy. The miner, whom they had already heard at his work, through the immense partition-wall, — or "pillar," as it is called, — was standing on a pile of rubbish driving his drill horizontally into the face of the coal-seam near the top. The laborer was separating the large fragments of coal from the slate, and the boy was sitting on a heap, separating the smaller pieces. They cast the slate aside, and threw the coal into a car, which had been drawn in on the track to the end of the chamber to be loaded.

In another chamber they found the miner working in under the seam. He was several feet beyond the face of it, and the top part hung over him and his little lamp like a tremendous ledge of black rock. It was so low that he could not stand erect. The boys, stooping, went in where he was at work.

"I have just this corner to blow out," he told

them; "then I shall put in a charge under the roof, and bring down all this coal overhead."

Lawrence asked if he did n't find it hard work to drill where he had to stoop so low.

"This is nothing," said the man. And he went on to tell how he had worked in coal-seams so thin that the miner could never stand upright, from the moment he entered his chamber till he left it. "I mined in one such," said he, "that pitched like the roof of a house. Imagine two steep roofs, one four feet above the other, and yourself getting out coal between them."

"How did you manage it? Did you work down from the top?"

"We worked up from the bottom. We kept the gangway below us, and run the coal down to it in chutes."

In another chamber they found the miner just preparing to blast. The boys retreated around the curve at the entrance, and waited for the fire to eat its way up through the fuse into the powder. Then came the explosion. Lawrence was expecting it, this time, and was not frightened; yet there was to his inexperienced nerves something fearful in the sudden concussion of air, which seemed to smite him with an angry buffet in the face and breast. The vast pillars of coal that upheld the hill seemed to tremble; and the roaring gust of sound swept on through the recesses of the mines.

VIII.

CURIOSITIES OF THE MINES.

In traversing the gangways and chambers, Lawrence noticed many places where there had evidently once been openings in the walls, but which were now closed. Some were boarded up, and some were built up with slabs of slate. Those on one side of the gangway, Owen said, were the entrances to old chambers that had been worked out and closed up. "Those on the other side are air-courses. They go through into another gangway, parallel to this. Wherever we run one gangway, look, we run another alongside of it. They are thirty feet apart. The chambers branch off to the right from the gangway we are in; and they branch off to the left from the other."

"Why do you run two gangways?"

"To get ventilation. You don't understand." Owen, in his eagerness to explain, dropped down in a half-sitting posture against the coal-pillar, and, taking a piece of chalk from his pocket, drew a white line down a leg of his trousers, while Lawrence held his little lamp, and Mr. Clarence and Muff looked on. "Now this is the gangway, look. Now this is the other gangway, look"; and he drew a parallel line. "Now these are the cross-cuts, or air-passages"; and he united the two with short chalk-lines drawn across from one to the other at intervals. "They are a hundred and twenty feet apart. Now here, on the

OWEN'S DIAGRAM.

opposite side from the air-courses, are the chambers. They sweep round the way they do, for the car-track must be curved; the cars could n't very well turn a square corner, look. The openings to the chambers are fifteen feet wide, with fifty-four feet of pillar between."

"Why so thick a pillar?"

"To hold the roof up. But the chambers branch

out, as you go in, till they leave only twenty foot of pillar between them. That 's as little as it is safe to leave. The wooden props just keep the roof of the chamber from falling; but the pillars are the main support. Rob them, and your whole roof is coming down, look!"

Lawrence did look, with a slight start, but perceived that his roof was safe and that Owen was merely illustrating a possibility.

"Now about the ventilation. Miners could n't live a day without that. The fire-damp would fill up the mines, and cause explosions. Then the powder-smoke and the breaths of so many men and mules would be stifling. So, in driving a gangway, you shall drive an air-course all the way beside it, — as they do in some mines, — or drive a parallel gangway, so as to send the air-current up one and down the other. You make this cross-cut, look, to let the air pass through. Then, when you get much beyond that, you open a new cross-cut, and close up the last one. In this way you keep on, closing up the cross-cuts behind you, so as to force the air always through the new one, near where you are at work. Then there are cross-cuts from one chamber to another, and the air is driven through them by shutting a door in the gangway. When the miner gets much beyond a cross-cut, he begins to suffer for air; so he opens another, and stops the last one."

Owen had by this time a rude diagram on his trousers, the black surface of which represented the coal, while the white lines and filling represented gangways, air-courses, and chambers. He now proceeded to show how the currents of air circulated through the mines, and were drawn out by means of the ventilating fan in the air-shaft.

Mr. Clarence meanwhile looked on somewhat superciliously. "Just lend me your trousers-leg and piece of chalk a minute," he said, giving his cane to Muff to hold. "That" — pointing at Owen's diagram — "is an absurd system of mining and ventilation. Now this is my uncle's system." Using the Welsh boy's patches for a blackboard, he prepared to demonstrate. "It saves a large part of this astonishing waste of coal left in the pillars, for one thing. And besides —"

At that moment Muff dropped the cane and darted with wild yelps into the darkness.

"What 's that?" cried Mr. Clarence, jumping up. "It must be a cat! He 's a terrible fellow for cats. If I don't look out, I shall lose him!"

"If he follows the cat, I know just where she 'll go," said Owen, putting his blackboards in lively motion, and following the dog that had followed the cat, while Lawrence and Mr. Clarence followed him.

He soon brought them to what Lawrence at first thought was a coal-chamber; but, on entering it, he found it was a stable. The floor was littered, and, ranged along by the wall, was a row of mangers, under one of which they found Muff, sure enough, barking at a hole where his game had found refuge.

"The cats down here are used to dogs," said Owen. "Here 's where they generally hide from 'em."

"Cats and dogs in the mines!" exclaimed Lawrence, "That is what I never expected to see."

"One of our miners has a dog that brings him his dinner. He comes to the head of the shaft at noon, with the pail in his mouth, and waits till a car is stopped for somebody going down; then he jumps aboard, and jumps out again at the foot of the shaft, and finds his way to the chamber where his master is, without any light, unless the mule-teams happen to be passing."

Lawrence was much interested in this and other dog-stories Owen and Clarence had to tell. But what was the use of cats in the mines?

"To kill off the rats," said Owen.

"You have rats down here too?"

"We used to have thousands of 'em. They got so thick one time, before we had cats, that they had no fear of you at all. They would fill a manger soon as ever you fed a mule, and go to eating right at his nose. You could take up a shovelful of 'em. You might kill as many as you pleased, there 'd be more the next time. They robbed the mules. So Mr. Lewis says one day, — he 's the inside foreman; we call the superintendent you saw the outside foreman; Mr. Lewis manages all the work in the mines, — he says one day, 'Boys,' he says, 'I 'll give any one of you a quarter, look, that will bring me a cat to-morrow.' So the next morning I puts a cat in a basket and ties the cover on, and comes down with her to see the fun when we let her out. At first she did n't know what to make of the strange place. But all at once she smells a rat, and gives a pounce, and comes out from under a manger growling and scuffling with a monstrous big rat in her mouth. Some other boys brought cats, and I bet the rats suffered! Now the cats are as much at home here as ever you saw cats anywhere. They seem to like the mines. They come purring and rubbing themselves around the miners, who always give 'em bits of their dinner. But the rats have just about disappeared."

Lawrence noticed that the mangers were covered with sheet-iron, which had been put on, Owen said, to prevent, not the rats, but the mules themselves, from gnawing the wood. "They 'd eat the mangers all up in a little while, if we did n't sheathe 'em. Look at this prop."

It was an oaken post as thick as Owen's body; and it had been so nearly gnawed in two, that a smart push with the hand might have broken it quite off. Several other props were in almost as bad a condition.

"I advise your foreman to have these props ironed," said Mr. Clarence. "If he don't, some of your uneasy mules will be playing the part of blind Samson, and pulling your house down."

Lawrence asked whether the stables were intended merely as a dining-hall for the mules, or whether they were kept in them over night.

"We stable them here all winter," said Owen. "The hostler comes down and feeds 'em. The blacksmith comes down and shoes 'em. The doctor comes down and doctors 'em, if they are sick. But in summer we stable 'em outside. They are going out now," said Owen, leading the way back to the gangway.

A train of mules was passing, with boys on their backs, stooping on the animals' necks as they passed under low portions of the roof. Other boys — door-keepers or slate-pickers — were following on foot, calling out, "Wait and give me a ride!" "Take me on, after you get outside!" with other like hopeful phrases, all aiming to establish comfortable relations between the mules' backs and the legs of the pursuing boys.

Owen described the characters of some of the mules as they passed. "That one with the muzzle on bites. That other one kicks — look out! That last kicked up and threw three boys over his head the other day; he thought two on his back was enough."

"How many mules are there?"

"Twenty, besides them that belong to the water-cars."

"Now my young friend will want to know what water-cars are for," said Mr. Clarence, bringing Muff away in his arms.

Owen soon had an opportunity of showing. They came to what he called a "basin," where the coal-bed lay lower than the foot of the shaft and the main gangways. It was like a hollow between hills, in which a pond of water settles, too low to be drained off. Here some men and boys were at work bailing. They dipped up the water into cars having tank-like boxes, which, when filled, were drawn up to the top of the hill," as Owen said,— properly enough, though it sounded oddly to Lawrence to hear him talk of a hill two hundred and fifty feet below the surface of the ground. The water was there emptied out, where it would run down the other slope of the gangway towards the shaft.

"Drainage," observed Mr. Clarence, "is of quite as much importance in coal-mining as ventilation. If it was n't for that, all these drifts and chambers would soon be full of water. I wish I had time, and I 'd show you my uncle's beautiful system!" He felt in his pocket for the piece of chalk, at the same time casting wistful glances at Owen's inviting trousers-legs. But it was getting too late for demonstrations on the blackboard.

"Mr. Lewis is going to rig a little steam pump, and force the water up the hill," said Owen. "He 'll bring the steam all the way from the engine-room in pipes, and run a little bit of an engine down here, that will save the labor of four men and four mules, day and night."

"But we are a long way from the shaft, are n't we?" said Lawrence, who thought, by the distance they had travelled, they must be at least a mile from it.

"Only about six hundred feet," said Owen. "The gangways make a circuit. We have been coming round towards the point we started from. Now you shall go up into the Diamond Vein, and see how

Mr. Lewis is managing to drain the low part of that."

"How do we get into it?" Lawrence asked, remembering that it was thirty feet above their heads.

Owen answered by leading the way to a low, narrow passage, which sloped up from the gangway and the lower coal-seam into strata of clear slate. This, Owen said, was a tunnel which Mr. Lewis had lately had constructed, as an avenue of communication between the two coal-beds. It started from what he called the top of the hill, in the lower bed, and went across, by a gentle ascent, to the bottom of the corresponding hill in the upper bed. To explain this, Owen had to

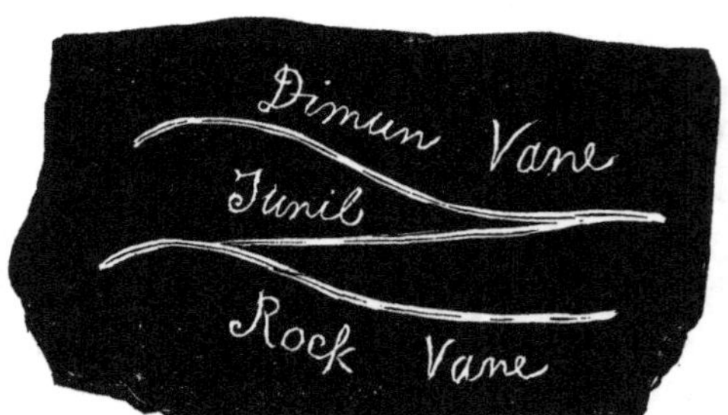

stop and chalk out a diagram on a slab of slate; by which means he succeeded in conveying the idea quite clearly, although, when he came to write in words to indicate the places of the *tunnel*, and the *Diamond* and *Rock Veins*, he showed himself somewhat less familiar with the spelling-book than with the mines.

"Look here," said Mr. Clarence, examining the jagged walls of the tunnel, which were pure argillaceous slate (or slate that had once been clay), beneath the Diamond Vein. "You can see the broken ends of fossil roots."

"The slate here was full of such," said Owen. "Sometimes great big roots — only not roots, look, but stone — would come out, all perfect."

Lawrence had thought that he already understood how the forests which made the coal-beds had their roots in underlying beds of clay; but now the fact became as it were a visible reality to him, and he was for a moment lost in wonder at Nature's vast and mysterious operations. "How long ago," thought he, "these immense forests must have been growing and decaying! How useless they must have seemed, — if there had been anybody on the earth then to think about them! And now, after ages and ages, here they are in great, thick layers of coal, for the use of man, at a time when he needs it, and could n't, as I see, do without it." Lawrence was not a particularly pious boy, but somehow a deep still sense of Infinite Love and Wisdom, — a Divine Providence, — forming and governing the world, stole over him, like a shadow of invisible wings.

He inquired if the coal of the two veins was of precisely the same quality. Owen said not quite, though they were both first-rate white-ash veins. Mr. Clarence said that the coal of no two beds anywhere was precisely the same, — though anthracite did n't show, by any means, such decided differences as the soft kinds did. "Some anthracite is very gassy, and some makes clinkers, or is full of slate and bone; while some burns without throwing off much gas, and leaves little besides ashes in the grate."

Then Lawrence wished to know the difference between white and red ash coal; and Mr. Clarence replied that red-ash was simply anthracite containing a small percentage of oxide of iron, or iron rust, which gave to its ashes their peculiar color. He went on to discourse in a quite learned way about the widely different varieties of bituminous coal, — how some would melt and run together, or "cake," in the fire; how some, containing perhaps quite as much bitumen, would not "cake," and were consequently considered more valuable for most purposes; how one sort yielded the largest amount of coal-oil, and another the largest amount of illuminating gas; how cannel-coal was probably so named because it burned with such a beautiful, clear flame, like a candle, or *cannel*, — as the word is pronounced in the Lancashire dialect, in England, and so forth, — the young gentleman talking loudly amidst the noise of a torrent that poured down through the tunnel from the upper coal-vein.

"It was mostly for the water that Mr. Lewis had this tunnel cut through," said Owen, as soon as he could get a chance to slip in a word. "When he first took charge of the mines, a few years ago, he found twenty-six men bailing water, up in this Diamond Vein, like those you saw below. The first thing he said was, 'Stop spending so much money that way.' Of course he knew the chambers would fill with water; but he said, 'Let 'em fill.' He just stopped work in 'em, and blew out the tunnel, look; and now he is driving a new gangway around behind the chambers, to tap 'em."

Into this new gangway Owen conducted his friends, after having shown them the old gangway and the chambers filled with water.

They had not proceeded far when they saw a lamp moving through the darkness before them.

"There 's Mr. Lewis himself!" cried Owen. "Quick! and you 'll see him tap a chamber."

Eager to know what tapping a chamber was, Lawrence hurried on with Mr. Clarence after their guide, and soon came up with the "inside foreman," just as he was entering a short new chamber which had been driven up from the new gangway so as to strike the end of one of the old chambers.

They found him to be a plain, sensible, pleasant Welshman; and he took a good deal of pains to explain to them what he was going to do.

"The old chambers, understand, are full of water. They pitch towards the bottom of the basin; and as soon as we stopped bailing they filled. Now I come directly to the bottom of the basin with the tunnel, and work this new gangway around by the lower end of the drowned chambers. Before, the water had to be drawn in cars up one slope, and poured down another; but now I make it travel with its own legs, down through the tunnel and the Rock Vein, direct to the shaft. That saves the work of many men and mules. You see this plug."

The boys saw it, — a large round stick of wood, driven near the bottom of the wall of coal, at the end of the new chamber.

"It stops a hole that has been drilled through into one of the drowned chambers. It would n't do, understand, to break through and let all the water out at once; it would flood everything. So we drill holes, and plug 'em, and then draw off the water by degrees. Now I unplug this. In a day or two I unplug another; and so on, till we get rid of all the water, without giving the pump at the shaft too much to do at once. Step back, or you 'll be spattered."

So saying, he loosened the plug with his foot, and pulled it out. It was followed by a jet of water, the gushing force of which indicated the powerful pressure on the other side. It shot out horizontally from the aperture, fell in a gentle curve, and, plashing into a channel cut for it, added its tribute to the torrent pouring down through the tunnel.

Returning from the Diamond Vein, Lawrence asked why they could not go up by one of the shaft-cars, which Owen had said stopped there.

"Because the cars have done running by this time," replied the little Welshman.

"Then how are we to get out of the mines, if we can't go up the shaft?"

TAPPING A CHAMBER.

"I 'll show you," said Owen, mysteriously.

Lawrence reflected that there must be a way out for the mules, besides the shaft, and said nothing.

They were in the Rock Vein again, passing an air-course, when Owen stopped.

"Here was a man killed the other day," said he. "There was fire-damp here; and he went in with his lamp."

"Fire-damp," said Mr. Clarence, anticipating Lawrence's question, "is what men of science" ("like myself," his manner seemed to say) "call light carburetted hydrogen; it is a gas composed of one part carbon and two parts hydrogen. The fissures of the coal formation are full of it. It shoots out of what we call blowers. It is much more plentiful and dangerous in the soft-coal mines than it is here; but one has to be careful about it here."

"Every mine has a fire-boss," said Owen. "He goes around every morning with a safety-lamp, and tests all the places where the fire-damp is likely to be. If he finds it safe to go in, he marks on the pillar with chalk. Here 's one of his marks, now."

"The safety-lamp" — Mr. Clarence took Lawrence's lamp in his hand to illustrate — "is constructed on the principle that flame will not pass through very small holes. It is simply a lamp surrounded by a fine wire gauze. This the gas-inspector, as we call him, — or fire-boss, as Owen calls him, — carries through the mines, holding it up under the roof where the fire-damp, which is lighter than common air, is always to be found, if anywhere. It goes to the top of the mines, just as water goes to the bottom, and stands in inverted puddles, where it can't flow away. It is invisible, of course, till you light it. If the safety-lamp passes through it, it takes fire inside of the wire; sometimes it puts the lamp out, and burns with a curious flame by itself, floating in the top of the gauze covering. The gas that gets in will burn, but the burning gas can't get out; it is caged. Some mines, especially some British coal-mines, are so gassy that the miners have to use safety-lamps altogether, and protect themselves still further, by very ingenious arrangements, against other deadly gases that fall to the bottom of the chambers."

"Our men won't work where there 's fire-damp," said Owen. "They 're afraid of it as they are of lightning. When they find it, they beat it down from the roof with old coats, or bags; then the air-current carries it off."

"I should like to see some of it burn," said Lawrence.

"That 's what a man said the other day. My father knew where there was just about a hatful of it in a little hollow of the roof, in an old air-course. So he says, 'You take the lamp, and put it up there, and you 'll find some.' So the man went feeling along with the lamp, till, the first thing he knew, the whole air before his eyes burst into a blaze; it knocked him down, and skinned his nose for him."

"A little hatful of gas expands like that!" cried Lawrence.

"That 's the danger," said Owen. "Suppose there is a foot of fire-damp up there now. You shall put up your lamp, look! It catches, and you shall multiply it by seven; it makes seven foot of solid blaze, look!"

"In the Mount Pleasant Mine, over here," Owen went on, "there was lately a terrible explosion. One morning the miners would n't wait for the fire-boss, and they went into a drift where there was gas. Eleven boys and eleven mules got killed. The fire-damp blowed 'em out of the drift, just like it had been a keg of powder. Then the air rushing back blowed 'em in again. They were all torn to pieces, so you could n't tell one from another."

"Accidents are the constant dread of miners' families," said Mr. Clarence.

"Just along here," said Owen, as they travelled on, "a boy got hurted the other day. He fell under a car. I was outside at the time. As soon as it got out that there had been an accident, you should have seen! The way the women and children came running to the shaft was something pitiful. There was hundreds there in a few minutes, wringing their hands, asking questions, — 'Who is it? who is it?' for every one thought it might be her own husband, or son, or father, till the boy was brought out."

"Was he badly hurt?"

"He died in a few days. He was a poor woman's only son. Mr. Lewis got up a subscription for her, and every miner gave something. It was very sad," said Owen, his voice choking a little. "Though sometimes there's a funny accident, look!" he added, making haste to be cheerful again. "At the Mount Pleasant Mine they have a slope twelve hundred feet long. An engine draws up the cars out of the mines by a rope. The other day a boy wanted to go down and carry his father's dinner. He pushed off a car, and got into it; but he forgot to hook the rope to it first. The car went like lightning, after it got well started, run off the track, and smashed all to bits. But the boy was n't hurted scarcely any. When the men picked him up all he said was, — he stuttered a little, look, — 'The engineer l-l-let me down too f-f-fast!' "

"Look here, young man," said Mr. Clarence. "Your lamps are almost out."

"So are we," said Owen. "Here 's the mules' gangway. This is a new thing, too. Mr. Lewis had it cut through, because he thought if the shaft should get afire, the men would all perish, if they did n't have some way to get out. Then it helps ventilation, and is handy for the mules. Before this was cut, every mule had to be brought down the shaft; and there was always danger of the colts breaking loose and jumping out of the cars."

Lawrence's lamp was burning so low that now the current of fresh air rushing down the gangway blew it out. The oil was getting low in Owen's lamp too; it scarcely lighted their way.

"What if we had lost our lights somewhere away off in the mines?" said Lawrence.

"I did so once," said Owen. "I was on my way to the shaft, to take the last car up. I came to some water so deep I did n't like to walk through it. So I got some stones and threw in, to step on. As I was throwing the last one, I gave my head a toss, look! and off went my lamp into the water. The mines were full of rats, and I was scared. I thought I might have to spend the night with 'em; and I knew they were hungry enough to eat me. I began to travel. I did n't mind stepping into the water then. I shouted, but could n't make anybody hear. I thought the last men must be going up the shaft by that time; and of course they would n't think to ask for me. That was before this gangway was cut through. I felt my way, and got along as fast as I could. All to once I saw a light. It was Mr. Lewis; he was around, looking after things, as he always is. So I went out with him, and bid good night to the rats."

"How cool the fresh air is!" said Lawrence. "I had n't thought of the mines being so warm. We shall see daylight soon."

"No, you won't," said Owen, — "though you may see starlight."

He was right. The in-rushing draught of air grew colder and colder, as they went up through the mule-trampled mud of the low, narrow, ascending gangway; and at last a faint light shone in at the entrance, which reminded Lawrence of the light Sindbad the Sailor saw at the end of his cavern. But it was not the light of day. The sun had gone down, and evening had come on, since they entered the mines.

They emerged from the low-roofed passage, — which was supported by a cribbing of timber, beyond the natural roof of rock, — and came out in the shadow of a bleak hillside. There was a noise of murmuring waters, — a dark river rushed by at their feet. Lights twinkled in the city beyond, and above them the stars shone.

"Here 's the Lackawanna. We have come out on its banks," said Owen. "The colliery building, where you went into the shaft, is away up on the hill yonder."

"I can't tell you how much obliged I am to you, Owen!" said Lawrence. "If you ever come to Massachusetts, I 'll try and do as much for you. In the mean time, I want to give you something to remember me by. I have n't anything but this pocket-knife; it 's small, but there 's first-rate stuff in the blades."

"I shall not take that from you!" said Owen; yet his hand opened involuntarily as the knife approached it, and closed again very quickly the moment it touched his palm, — for Owen was but a boy, and it was not in boy-nature to refuse such a gift.

"Now I wish I could see the superintendent and thank him," said Lawrence.

But Owen said it was too late to find him at the office. Then Lawrence remembered his uncle, who he feared might be growing anxious about him; and Mr. Clarence said they ought to be on their way back to the hotel. So Owen piloted them up the hill to the track of the street-cars, where they took leave of him, as if they three had been old friends, — Mr. Clarence also slipping something into the willing Welsh palm.

A street-car came along, and stopped for them; and Lawrence, getting into it, with Mr. Clarence and Muff, rode back to the hotel, where the two boys found their respective uncles, just returned, stepping out of the buggy at the door.

CHAPTER V.

AMONG THE IRON-MEN.

I.

LETTER-WRITING UNDER DIFFICULTIES.

"WHAT 's the programme for this evening?" said Mr. Clarence, as he entered the reading-room of the hotel with his new friend after supper.

With his cane under his arm, and a toothpick in his mouth, and his hat tipped gayly upon one side of his head, he was looking quite fresh and spirited, after the day's adventures. So, too, was Lawrence, though his manner was by no means so light and airy as that of his vivacious friend. No one, to have seen them after their thorough washing and brushing and refreshment, would have suspected that they had so lately come out of a coal-mine.

"I think," said Lawrence, "I 'll write a letter to my little coz, and tell her about the mines and the miners, and how I made your acquaintance."

"Capital!" said Mr. Clarence. "And I believe I 'll write to *my* little coz, and tell her about *you*."

So the young gentlemen got some note-paper and pens, and seated themselves at the table, the showy Mr. Clarence on one side and the more solid-looking Lawrence opposite him, with a very large inkstand between them. They shoved the newspapers aside, dipped their pens (Mr. Clarence said it was like dipping into a well), and then dated their letters.

"*Scranton, October*," wrote Mr. Clarence, with a characteristic flourish, and then stopped. "What 's the day of the month?"

Lawrence told him, and in his turn inquired whether Pennsylvanians wrote the abbreviation of the name of their State *Penn.* or *Pa.*

"We write it both ways; it is the same thing," said Mr. Clarence; adding, with a comical smile, "*Penn* was the *Pa* of this State, you know; and that 's the reason of it, I suppose."

"You made me laugh, and joggled me," said Lawrence, throwing aside the sheet he had begun on, and taking another.

Mr. Clarence began to flourish again, but stayed his hand before touching pen to paper.

"I never wrote to my little coz in my life. How do you start off?"

"*My dear little Cousin Ethel,* — that 's my style," said Lawrence, writing.

"Tip-top! You are my Complete Letter-Writer. *My — dear — little — Cousin — Eth—* No! hold on! My cousin's name is Jessie. Now *I* shall have to take a new sheet. *My dear little Cousin Jessie,* — that 's all right; a fine opening, as the miners say. Now which way do you carry your drift? In other words, what next?"

Lawrence scratched his ear and looked solemnly at

the great inkstand. Mr. Clarence looked cheerfully at Lawrence. Then Lawrence read over the first line of his letter,—*My dear little Cousin Ethel,*—*My dear little Cousin Ethel,*"—three or four times,—something like a fisherman trolling his line for a bite, hoping that an idea would rise and hook itself on at the end of it. He could think of things enough to write, but could n't get hold of just the right thing first. It may be added that the consciousness of his friend's eyes upon him did not help him much.

"I 've a plan!" said Mr. Clarence at last. "We 'll both write the same things to our dear little cousins. You think of a sentence, and we 'll both write it; then I 'll think of one, and give you the benefit. Division of labor, you know."

"Well, you think of a sentence first."

"How 's this? *My dear little*, and so forth: *I have to-day made the acquaintance of a splendid young fellow,*—which means you."

"But when I write it 't will mean you," said Lawrence, laughing.

"In that way we shall make an even thing of the compliments. I don't object to being called a splendid young fellow; do you? Have you got it down?"

"I 've written it *capital fellow,*—did you say *splendid?*"

"Never mind. Don't change it. Only underline *capital,* so as to make it even. What 's your sentence?"

"*His pleasant face is before me while I write,*" suggested Lawrence.

"Excellent! Don't you see how admirably it works? Only — will a slight amendment be in order?"

"Certainly."

"Then permit me to suggest that we might employ a rather stronger epithet than *pleasant face;* might n't we? Suppose we make it *handsome face?* Can you conscientiously?"

Lawrence thought he could, but laughed so that he did not trust his hand to write for about a minute. Then he noticed that he had already written *pleasant.*

"Never mind, make it *pleasant and handsome;* I think I can stand it," said Mr. Clarence. "*He is here in company with his uncle, the distinguished* — Here write in the names of our respective uncles. Now it 's your turn again."

"*And while his uncle and mine are talking of the business that brought them here, in the corner* —" Lawrence went on.

"Brought them here in the corner?" queried Mr. Clarence. "That don't sound just right."

"I mean, while they are talking in the corner about the business that — But it 's a bad sentence, any way. I 'm afraid I never can write a decent letter in this way."

"Yes, you can. Push ahead! Don't you know the secret of fluent composition? It 's this: never stop to think. If you stop to think, you 're lost."

Just then the little dog Muff jumped up on the table, and scrambling over the newspapers, stretched his chin out on his fore-paws between the two friends, with his nose near the inkstand.

"I never can go on with that wagging tail before my eyes!" said Lawrence.

"In other words, you think our letter-writing will be curtailed," said Mr. Clarence.

"I think Muff will be responsible for the final paws we have come to," replied Lawrence, — for that is the way with young fellows: if one makes a pun his companion is sure to feel called upon to match it, if not with a fresh one, then with one not quite so fresh.

"Here, Muff! hold our pens while we scratch our heads for ideas," said Mr. Clarence.

The dog took the pens by the handles, and held them with all the gravity of a lord chancellor, while the two letter-writers scratched industriously for the ideas that did not come. Soon Lawrence leaned his head on the table, pillowing it on his arms. The truth is, he was tired and sleepy. Mr. Clarence followed his example; and there they sat, or rather lay, head to head, with their elbows squared at each other and with the inkstand and the lord chancellor between them. In three minutes they were fast asleep.

At the end of about an hour Lawrence lifted his head with remarkable suddenness, opened his eyes very wide, and looked wildly about him. Mr. Clarence, with his head still down, and with cataracts of hair over his arms, was gently snoring. There was nobody else in the room, except the lord chancellor, and he, too, had fallen into a snooze, with his muzzle on his paws, and with the pens beside it on the table.

"Hello!" said Lawrence.

"Hello!" said Mr. Clarence, starting up and tossing back the cascade of hair from his face, wide awake in an instant.

"I thought I was chasing rats in a coal-mine, and had got my face in a mule's manger, and could n't get it out," said Lawrence, feeling his neck, which had suffered.

"I did n't imagine you were asleep!" said Mr. Clarence. "I was n't; I 've been thinking what to write."

"You were snoring, any way."

"O no! I make that noise in my head sometimes when I am thinking pretty hard. It 's the rumbling of the mill, you know." And the miller arranged his tangled hair. He was one of those persons who can never be convinced that they have slept on irregular occasions; and Lawrence let the matter pass with a laugh.

"It 's after nine; you have been thinking over an hour. Where are our uncles?"

"Oh! they? They have walked out," said Mr. Clarence, glancing about the room. "This seems to be letter-writing under difficulties. Let 's walk out too. I am as much refreshed as if I had had a nap. Come, Muff!" taking the lord chancellor under his arm. "He 's a dog of steady habits. Goes to bed early. The porter will take care of him while we go in search of adventures."

Muff having been disposed of, the young gentlemen walked out of the hotel arm in arm. It was a still, moonlight evening. The streets were almost deserted. Mr. Clarence looked up at the sky with a sentimental air, and said, pensively, —

"Behold the moon! how she spreads her silver mantle over the silent world! Did you ever think of it? She has shone upon the earth just so thousands of nights before, and where were you and I? She will shine just so again, a year from now, — ten years from now, — a hundred years from now, — and where will you and I be? O moon! I pause for a reply," added Mr. Clarence, theatrically.

He did not pause a great while, however (the moon evidently having no intention whatever of replying), but said presently, —

"I'll tell you where let's go! To the iron-works! — to see the blast-furnaces by night!"

II.

THE BLAST-FURNACES BY NIGHT.

LAWRENCE eagerly accepted the suggestion. They walked briskly up the street, and soon came in sight of the flaming furnace throats, and of the black figures of workmen passing to and fro before them.

The furnaces of the Lackawanna Iron-Works are

built on the side of the steep right bank of Roaring Brook. They are large and tall; their immense foundations are laid in the foot of the bank, while their throats roar and flame over its summit fifty feet above. It was at that elevation, on a sort of high, dim platform, that the lads saw the human figures defined against the glow of the fires.

"They 're feeding the furnaces up there," said Mr. Clarence.

The boys found a cart-track which took them up a short slope to an open shed, covering great piles of what appeared to be stones and rocks and anthracite coal. A gang of laborers were at work shovelling up these materials and wheeling them off in small iron carriages. The rocks in some of the piles were in rough blocks, just as they came from the quarries; but in others they seemed to have been broken up into sizes suitable for making macadamized roads. It was from these latter piles, and from the piles of coal, that the carriages were filling; and the lads, watching the men, saw that they wheeled their loads directly into the glare of the furnace throats, which lighted up the scene.

"This is certainly stone!" said Lawrence, picking up a fragment from a pile where a man was shovelling.

"Sure it is," said the man, — "limestone."

"What do you do with it?"

"Cast it in with the charge."

"What is the charge?"

"Go with that carriage, and you will see."

Another laborer coming with an empty carriage left it, and, taking the one the shovellers had just filled, wheeled it out across the platform. The lads followed, advancing into the terrible heat and glare of the furnace throats.

The furnaces were four in number; but only their tops were here visible, — huge, funnel-shaped necks, somewhat higher than a man's head, ranged along the edge of the platform, above the roof of the casting-house which enclosed the bodies of the furnaces below. There were iron doors in the sides of the funnels; into these the contents of the carriages were cast; and through these, as also through the circular openings in the funnel-tops, roared the flames, as if spouted from nose and mouth by so many young volcanoes.

Lawrence was at first almost terrified at the position in which he found himself. He looked down into the fiery gulf into which the man dumped his load with a loud clang of the iron carriage striking the iron plates. There the furnace enlarged like a yawning crater below its comparatively narrow throat. At first he could see only an abyss of many-colored, dazzlingly beautiful flames; but presently he could distinguish, heaped high in the midst of them, and only a few feet lower than the charging-plates on which he stood, the top of a dark mound. It was composed of the freshly dumped materials from the piles under the shed. Around and over them, and through every chink between the lumps, the flames swept and darted and surged.

CHARGING THE FURNACES.

Another laborer came, and dumped a carriage-load of coal —great lumps of anthracite—into the throat. Then a third came with a load of what seemed another kind of stone. Then the door was closed.

"But this is n't stone!" cried Lawrence, seizing a lump, and retreating with it from the intolerable glare of the fire. "This must be the ore."

"Ore it certainly is," said Mr. Clarence. "Ore, limestone, coal,—they all go into the furnace together, as you see."

"How, then, is the iron ever separated from the earthy matters?" said Lawrence, puzzled and astonished. "I should think it would be full of ashes and dirt. And what is the use of the limestone?"

"Perhaps we can find some person who will tell us," said Mr. Clarence. "But look here!"

They had retreated to the edge of the platform. They were on a spot which overlooked the roofs of buildings below, and the firelit waters of Roaring Brook pouring over a high dam, in a beautiful cascade, and rushing along their rocky bed under steep ledges, in light and shadow, at the base of the hill. Surrounding this bright flame-picture was the still, moonlit night, silvering peacefully the country and the town. Lawrence thought he had never looked upon so strikingly wild and picturesque a scene, and he stood gazing at it wonderingly until Mr. Clarence pulled him away.

"Ask one of these men about the limestone," said Mr. Clarence, as they returned to the shovellers at one of the piles. And he himself put the question in his polite way.

"The loimestone?" said the man, staring at him. "Why, we could n't do onything, mon, but for the loimestone."

"But what 's the use of it?"

"The use of it? The use, when we could n't get a blast without it! It 's loike ahsking the use of the air ye breathe."

"I know something of the use of the air we breathe: it gives oxygen to the blood," said Lawrence. "Now what does the limestone do to the furnace?"

"Mayhap it gives what ye call oxengin to the furnace loike," said the man, grinning with his hard face over his short stump of a pipe; and he returned to his shovelling with the air of one who had rendered a reason.

"I can tell you what you want to know," said another laborer, leaning on his shovel. "The limestone physics the furnace." But that was hardly a satisfactory explanation.

Another said, "The lime helps the flow of the iron."

A fourth said, "It makes the flux."

"No doubt, my friends," said Mr. Clarence. "But there 's more in it than all that. We 'll find out by and by. Let 's take a look at the boilers."

There were twenty of these, and they were ranged in order over an extensive fire-chamber, a door of which was opened by a good-natured attendant, that the visitors might look in. No fuel was visible, but billows of flame filled the space, undulating far away out of sight, under the boilers, which they enveloped.

"Where do the flames come from?" Lawrence asked, surprised at the beautiful display.

"From the furnaces," said the man. "They are a part of the waste heat."

"Then it don't all come out of the furnace throats?"

"Only a little of it. Below the throats are flues, which you can't see. There are pipes from the flues that bring some of the heat here. The rest of it goes to the hot-blast ovens."

"What are those?"

"The chambers where the cold air is heated before it is driven into the furnaces. It would n't do to drive in such a quantity of air cold."

"It would cool the furnaces," suggested Lawrence.

"Besides," added Mr. Clarence, "cold air don't burn like hot air. Hot air strikes the gases, and makes instantaneous combustion. But cold air has to get partly heated before it burns much; and they could n't begin to get so intense a heat with it."

"But I don't understand yet the use of the boilers," said Lawrence.

"Why," said Mr. Clarence, "the boilers drive the engines, that drive the fan, that drives the air, that drives the fires and makes the blast. They are blast-furnaces, you know."

"Where they make flint-glass," replied Lawrence, "they have tall chimneys, by which they get draught enough without any such apparatus."

He had no idea of the power of the blast until he went to look at the engines. There were four, of one thousand horse-power each. The immense fly-wheels ("They regulate the motion of the machinery, you know," said Mr. Clarence) almost completely filled the space between the floor and the roof of the building. The weight of the largest of them, the engineer said, was forty thousand pounds. The silence and swiftness of these huge, whirling wheels was something wonderful. "And is n't it curious to think of that quiet man with the newspaper being the master of all this tremendous machinery?" said Lawrence.

"Yes; man is little, but he is the trump-card on this planet," replied Mr. Clarence.

The air was forced by the engines through huge iron pipes, — "blowing cylinders," the engineer called them, — and such was the power of the blast that it entered the furnaces under a pressure of eight or nine pounds to the square inch.

"Think of a tall chimney making a draught equal to that!" said Mr. Clarence. "A chimney would have to be powerful enough to lift itself up by the straps of its boots! Iron is n't glass; and you see the smelting furnace has to be constructed on an entirely different principle. Now let's go down to the casting-house."

III.

THE CASTING-HOUSE.

HALF-WAY down the hillside, they passed a large reservoir of water, its still surface lit up like a little lake, by the furnace fires above. Farther on they descended a steep flight of steps to the roadway between the base of the hill and Roaring Brook. Along this road was laid an iron track for cars, leading into the casting-house.

This was a spacious, high-raftered, depot-like building, open on the side of the brook. On the other side were massive piers of masonry supporting the great furnaces. In the shadowy background could be seen the iron pipes that brought down the hot-air blast. In front of each furnace was an enclosed space filled with sand,—something like the arena of a circus, except that it was divided into two "floors" by a passage-way running down the centre. One of the floors in each arena appeared to be ready for casting, being laid out in regular, smooth channels, as if careful impressions of a gigantic gridiron had been taken in the deep, fine sand. The other floors were either in a tumbled condition, just as the iron of the last casting, when taken up, had left them, or laborers were engaged in laying down in them the wooden patterns by which the gridiron impressions were made. The sand was shovelled upon these, and packed about them; and it seemed to be just moist enough to retain the mould, in clean, handsome shape, after they were removed.

"Those are the pig-beds," said Mr. Clarence. "Of course you have heard of iron pigs! Well, this is where they are littered. Here are, in each of these floors, eight or ten pig-beds. To each bed there is what they call a sow. That 's the main channel that runs across the floor. You 'll see presently how that nourishes the pigs," — for Mr. Clarence saw by the signs that the men were preparing to cast.

A gang of a dozen or more were lounging about the hearth of one of the furnaces, leaning on iron bars, or sitting on benches, as if waiting for something. The boys went up where they were, and asked how long before they were going to cast.

"In a few minutes," said one. "We are just waiting for the fellers to come down with the word from up above. You 'd better keep back on the far side. You 'll see better there, and be out of danger."

The boys accordingly withdrew to the foot of the arena, on the side of the brook, — Mr. Clarence smiling at the idea of danger, but saying, airily, "We shall be out of the way, though."

They turned to look at the brook; and Lawrence noticed that there were cavernous openings in the steep ledges opposite, into which the waters rushed.

"Those are old coal-openings," said Mr. Clarence; "for here was a good coal-mine once. But it got on fire, and burnt I don't know how long, till they turned the brook into it and put it out."

The "fellers" had now come down from "up above"; and there were forty or fifty men in the casting-house. Then one who had been leaning on an iron bar grasped it with both hands, and began to drive it with sharp clicks against the hearth of the first furnace.

"He is drilling out the clay that stops the iron," said Mr. Clarence. "You 'll see it spirt soon!"

Just then a furious roaring sound filled the building.

"That is the blast; it is let off from the furnace when they cast."

At the same time sparks began to fly, and dazzling spatters of molten metal followed each stroke of the drill.

"It 's coming now!" cried Mr. Clarence, while Lawrence stood thrilled with expectation.

At the word out gushed the terrible molten torrent. The men were active and alert about it in an instant, shouting and springing to and fro, eager to guide and control the fearful flood. Some threw shovelfuls of sand upon it, to check its too rapid rush, while it poured down a channel prepared for it and began to fill the pig-beds in the upper part of the floor. It filled the mould of the "sow" first, then flowed down into the pigs, filling one after the other as it crept along. As soon as one pig-bed was filled, gates of clay, called "shutters," placed across the channel leading to it, were suddenly driven down by men with heavy sledge-hammers, and the fiery stream was turned into the next sow below. There was just slope enough to the floor to give a sufficient fall to

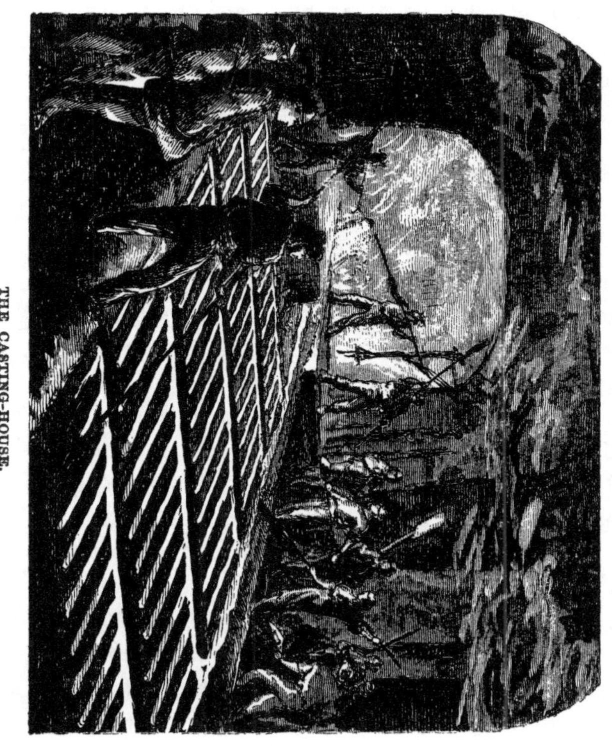

THE CASTING-HOUSE.

the running metal. Sand, as I have said, was thrown upon it, and the gates were driven down when it came too fast; and when it moved too sluggishly in any direction it was helped along by means of long, thin strips of wood or slender poles, which the men drew before it, very much as a child encourages a stream of water-drops by leading it with his finger. The poles were often on fire, and were as often quenched in the moist sand.

So floor after floor was cast, three of the furnaces being tapped in quick succession. The streams of molten metal lighting up the night, the sparks flying off from them and shooting hither and thither in little explosive showers, the flaming poles, the heat, the glare, the deafening roar of the blast, the animation of the workmen, their swift movements and loud cries, and finally the floors covered with enormous red-hot gridirons, and the sight of men walking quickly but unconcernedly over them, — all combined to make up a scene of the most vivid interest to the mind of Lawrence.

As soon as a floor was cast, sand was shovelled all over the beds of glowing metal; then water from a hose-pipe was thrown on copiously, filling the air with clouds of steam. Then men, stripped for the work, — naked to their waists, with clogs on their feet, — went on to the floors with sledges and levers, with which they broke up the iron while it was yet soft, separating the pigs from the sows, and dividing the sows into pig-shaped bars. (" Though I don't see why they were ever called pigs," Lawrence wrote afterwards to his little Cousin Ethel. "They don't look at all like young porkers, but are just rough pieces of cast-iron as big as my leg, and almost as tall, when they are stood up, as I am.")

"I should think you would suffocate," Mr. Clarence said to one of these men, who emerged from the stifling cloud and heat of one of the floors, and came out for a breath of air where the boys stood.

"I am used to it. I shall put all that iron on cars before midnight."

"How many pigs are there on that floor?"

"About three hundred. They weigh from a hundred to a hundred and twenty-five pounds apiece. As soon as they cool a little, I begin to handle them."

"Do you work all night?"

"No; my time is up when that job is done. There are two sets of hands; when this set goes off another comes on."

"How often do you cast?"

"Every six hours, day and night."

"How long after the ore is put in at the charging-doors above before it comes out melted iron?" Mr. Clarence inquired.

"Three days," said the man.

"And how much does one of those furnaces hold?"

"Six hundred tons of stock."

"That means coal, ore, and limestone, all together," said Mr. Clarence. "Six hundred tons, my lad!"

and he tapped Lawrence on the shoulder with his cane. "Can your glass-works beat that?"

"They are drawing off the iron again!" said Lawrence, seeing another stream of fiery liquid gushing from the furnace.

"That 's the cinder," said the man. "It comes from another opening higher up than the tapping-hole for the iron."

"Let 's go up and look at it," said Mr. Clarence.

They drew near and saw the dazzling stream pour down, through a channel prepared for it, to a spout, where it fell into a flaring pan as large as a cart-box, which had been brought up on a car, along a branch of the railway track, to receive it. When the pan was nearly full, the flow was stopped, and the car, loaded with the glowing mass, was drawn away by a mule.

Observing a person who seemed to be a sort of overseer, Lawrence asked him what the cinder was, and what it was good for.

"It is good for nothing. It is the slag."

"What is it made of? Ashes, for one thing, I suppose."

"Yes; but the limestone makes a good part of it."

"Now," said Mr. Clarence, in his polite way, "I see we have found an intelligent man; and perhaps he will kindly inform us what the limestone is used for."

"I can tell you a little. Do you know anything about the construction of a blast-furnace?" and, the boys confessing their ignorance, the speaker continued: "It is built up of fire-clay inside that solid stone-work, which is made very solid and strong, and bolted together, as you see, in order to support such a tremendous pressure. The furnace is shaped something like an egg standing on its big end. It is fifty feet high, from the hearth to the throat. It is eigh-

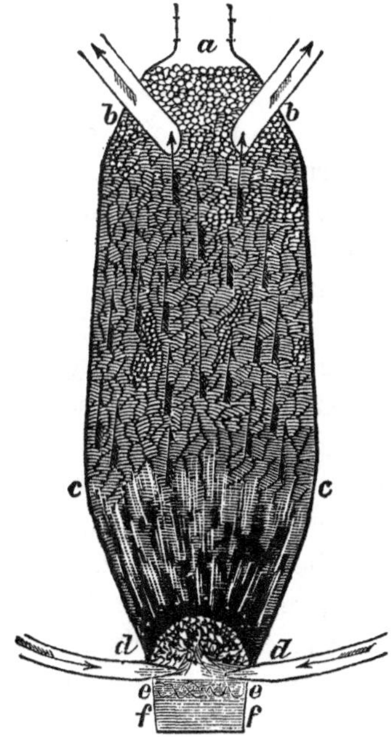

a, throat; *b*, *b*, flues; *c*, *c*, boshes; *d*, *d*, tweers; *e*, *e*, flux *f*, *f*, iron in the hearth.

teen feet broad in the boshes, — that is, through the thickest part of the egg. The materials thrown in have room to swell, as the heat expands them, and they settle down into the larger part. The hearth is the chamber, or reservoir, in the bottom of the furnace for receiving the melted metal and flux. Just over the hearth are the tweers; step here, and I will show you where the blast is driven in."

"Tweers! what a word! It must be from the French *tuyère*, which means a pipe," observed Mr. Clarence.

"Very likely, for it is a tapering aperture that receives the blast from the ends of these pipes, and carries it into the furnace. There are six of these tweers; and it is through these we blow the fires." And the man proceeded to explain the operation going on within the furnace.

"Crude iron ore," said he, "is always more or less oxidized; that is, it contains a quantity of oxygen. It also contains a good deal of earthy matter. Now, in the furnace, the ore soon begins to soften, and to part with its oxygen, which unites with the carbon of the coal, and with the oxygen of the air-blast helps make the fire. At the same time the ore absorbs carbon from the coal, which gives it the quality of cast-iron. The ore does not actually melt until it almost reaches the hearth. It is in a sort of pasty condition, when it comes within the direct influence of the blast; then it flows at once. The limestone begins to flow first, and it helps the flow of the iron. Then the iron, being the heaviest of all the materials in the furnace, goes to the bottom of the hearth, and everything else floats on top of it."

"I see now how it is separated from the ashes and other materials!" cried Lawrence. "It is by its own weight."

"That is it. But there is another thing; we have n't got through with the limestone yet. The melted lime makes the flux, which acts like a filter to the iron. The metal is at the bottom, and the flux floats on top of it, like oil upon water. Now every particle of iron that melts and comes down has to pass through this flux. If you could look in, you would see the melted metal trickling through it in drops, or little streams, something like rain falling through the air. The lime takes out the earthy impurities of the iron, and gathers the coal-ashes as they come down. To keep the flux in good condition, we have to draw it off, as it becomes loaded with impurities, and make room for fresh flux to fill its place. Here it comes out, as you see, in what we call slag, or cinder. The flux has still another use. Covering the melted metal as it does, it protects it from the continued direct action of the blast, which would soon oxidize it again, and make a different quality of iron."

"How much pig-iron do you make here in a year?"

"A thousand tons a week, — over fifty thousand tons a year."

"Where does your ore come from?"

"From New Jersey. It is dug out of the mountains, where it lies in beds all the way from two feet to thirty-five feet thick."

Lawrence thought he would like to visit the iron-mines. His curiosity was also excited with regard to the processes by which this coarse pig-iron was afterwards converted into all the various shapes and qualities of cast-iron, wrought-iron, and steel. But Mr. Clarence said, "I suspect our affectionate uncles would like to hear something about us by this time"; and, thanking their new acquaintance, while they took leave of him, they hastened back to the hotel.

Profile Plan (showing the ship as if sawed through the centre, from stem to stern).

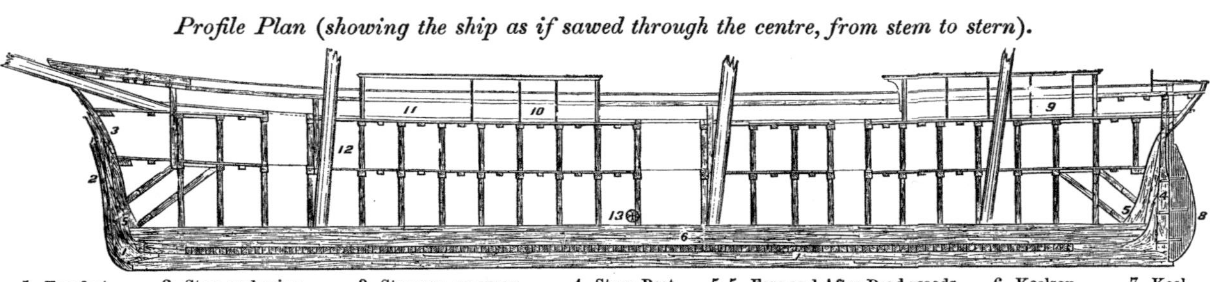

1. Forefoot. 2. Stem and gripe. 3. Stemson, or apron. 4. Stern-Post. 5, 5. Fore and After Dead-woods. 6. Keelson. 7. Keel. 8. Rudder. 9. Cabin. 10. Galley. 11. Forecastle. 12. Chain Locker. 13. Centre of Displacement.

Deck Plan (right-hand, or starboard side, shows the upper deck; left, or port side, the lower deck and timbers).

1. Fore Hatch. 2. Forecastle. 3. Store-room. 4. Galley. 5. State-room. 6. Main Hatch. 7. After Hatch. 8. State-rooms. 9. Captain's State-room. (Starboard side.) 10. Dining-room. 11. Fore Mast. 12. Main Mast. 13. Mizzen Mast.

CHAPTER VI.

AMONG THE SHIP-BUILDERS.

I.

THE SHIP-YARD.

THE next morning the two friends parted, Mr. Clarence going off with his uncle down the valley, and Lawrence returning with the doctor to their home in Massachusetts.

But the friendship thus formed was destined to continue; and a few weeks later we find Lawrence in Massachusetts, writing wonderfully long letters to Mr. Clarence in Pennsylvania. Having obtained from the writer authentic copies of these, we are enabled to finish the story of his adventures in his own words.

Here I am again (he wrote); and I am going to tell you about some of the things I have seen since I said good by to you that morning on the cars, — for this is what you made me promise I would do. I am not much used to writing letters, as maybe you remember; but my uncle says if I write just as I would talk, I shall do well enough, — only it must be about something I am interested in.

Well, what I am interested in just now is ships! You see, my uncle sent me over to East Boston the other day to find a man that moved away from here, and owed him a bill, — and I was to have the money if I collected it, which would be right handy about Christmas time, you know. But the man was n't at home; and while I was waiting for him, I thought I would take a stroll down by the water. It was a splendid day, — just cool enough; there was a fine breeze blowing, and sailing vessels and ferry-boats were passing in fine style; there was Charlestown and the Navy-Yard over opposite; and on the shore, right down before my eyes, was the skeleton of a big ship. I started for that. It was on the farther side of a great yard between the street and the water, — a yard full of great timbers and piles of lumber, and men at work chopping, measuring, hauling, and lifting; there was also a saw-mill and a sort of blacksmith shop.

I looked into the office as I passed the gate. It was a little square room, with two or three men in it talking earnestly over some drawings and figures on the desk, and a number of handsome ship-models, all nicely polished, fastened to the walls. Then there were framed pictures of steamers and ships under full sail. The room had quite a nautical look. I wanted to stop and ask about the models, but the men were busy, and so I walked on down into the yard.

I don't think you ever saw more chips on an acre of ground! There were old chips rotting in the dirt; fresh new chips just split off from the logs; and chips in every stage of youth and old age between. There was a wagon loading up with chips; there were women filling baskets with chips; there was a great staring sign, — "NO CHIPS TAKEN FROM THIS YARD"; and a stick of timber, which a horse was dragging off, went ploughing its way through dirt and chips. Burn it over, and could n't you raise corn and beans in that yard? I bet you!

I stopped to watch the men at work. One was hewing out a stick of timber to something like this shape. As he looked up and nodded at me, I asked

him what that stick was for. "That? That 's a futtick," said he. "What 's a futtick?" said I. "A part of a frame," said he. "What 's a frame?" said I. "A frame is a rib, — what you would call a pair of ribs. These timbers we are hewing out here, they 're all for frames," said he. "They are different shapes; no two exactly alike; and they are all cut out, just as you see, with the axe. We have these marks to go by."

Then I noticed the man who was making the marks. He had some thin boards sawed in just the shape he wanted the face of the timbers cut. He laid one of these flat on a hewed stick, and marked around the edges with a red pencil. Some of these boards — they are called moulds — were very long and curved only a little. Others were shorter, and curved very much more. Some were curved like a bow; others were almost straight, being curved only a little at one end. As there are some hundreds of timbers in the side of a big ship, and every timber has to have a separate mould, and as some of these moulds are made of two or three boards pieced together, you see it must take a good many boards, as well as a good deal of gumption, just to get the patterns ready, before even a timber is touched. Then here is another thing. Besides the shape given to the stick by the mould, which determines its up-and-down curve in the ribs of the ship, it must be hewed just right to fit in with the others, and make its part of the curved lines running lengthwise along the vessel's side. So most of the timbers have to be bevelled more or less. All the bevel angles come marked on a board, called a "bevel-board," and the carpenter takes off those, one by one, with his bevel instrument, and marks them on the ends of the sticks, for the choppers. And he must be careful to get the right bevel on the right stick. It is as if every bone in your body had to be designed and shaped separately, before you were put together; and that makes ship-building something wonderful, don't it? Though it is really the pieces of only one side that the architect has anything to do with. He designs the ribs on your right side, for instance. The moulds for one of these are just turned over, and the bevels reversed, to make the corresponding rib on your left side. Understand?

Your ribs are all of oak, as you must know. The best qualities of white or live oak are preferred, to build you stanch and strong. And the timber must be cut when the sap is out of it, and well seasoned afterwards, or you are liable to rot.

The most of the timber used in this yard, one of the men told me, comes from Virginia and Maryland. It is n't quite so good always as our Northern white oak, but it is cheaper. Oak in New England is getting to be a scarce article; but, since the war, whole forests in Virginia are bought up cheap, so that the expense of it here amounts to but little more than the cost of cutting and shipping it. Crews go out from our ports and spend the winter getting timber when the sap is down in the roots. They take out their oxen and cows, and sometimes their wives and babies, and build huts in the Southern forests, and have a merry time of it. Often they take out the moulds of a ship, and cut all her timbers into shape for building, on the spot; so that when they are landed here they are all ready to go into the frames. Think of a stick fitted there in the woods for a particular part of a particular rib of a particular ship to be built months afterwards, hundreds of miles away! There seemed to me something romantic about the voyages of these crews; and I thought I should like to go out with them, and spend a winter in the Virginia forests. But the chopper who told me this, and who has been out often, said he guessed I would find it hard.

They don't work much in these ship-yards during the winter, he told me. It is all out-door work. The storms interfere with it, and the snow is a great bother. "Sometimes you go out in the morning," he said, "and find every timber in the yard covered; and the stagings about the ship will be all slippery with snow and ice, — for it is n't often a common vessel is built under a house, like those over at the Navy-Yard." I looked across and could see the immense ship-houses standing with their ends towards the water. "This ship," said he, "won't be complete before December; and a good deal of snow will have to be shovelled for her, before ever she is launched."

II.

BUILDING THE SHIP.

I WAS in a hurry to see how the frames were put together; so I followed one of the timbers, which a horse was hauling away, and soon came to a high platform, to the top of which it was drawn up an inclined plane, by means of a rope and pulley.

I went up with it, stepping on cleats nailed across the planks on one side of the plane. Beyond was the half-finished skeleton of the ship that was building. The stern was towards the water, and the other end of the keel came up even with the platform. The keel was an immense stick of timber, — or rather several sticks pieced together, — perfectly straight and nearly two hundred feet long. It was laid on piles of blocks; and it slanted up a little from the end towards the water, so as to give the ship the proper inclination for launching. If the keel was laid level, she would n't slide off, you know.

The first thing I noticed was that the ribs were complete on both sides to the tops, as far as they were built at all. As I had seen a picture of a ship's ribs built up a little way all round, before the upper pieces were joined on, I had expected to see something like that here; but I learned that only small boats are made in that way, — though even large vessels used to be, fifty or a hundred years ago.

There the great ribs were, complete to about midships, and supported on the sides by two little groves of props. The part of the keel towards the platform was a naked piece of timber, — like half of your backbone waiting for the ribs to be fitted to it.

There were a dozen men on the platform; and now I saw what they were doing. They took the timbers as they came up from the yard, and put them together in a frame shaped like a big letter U. This was laid flat on the platform, with the bottom of the U toward the ship. The position it was designed for, near the middle of the keel, where the vessel is broadest and the bottom flattest, gave it its U shape. Near one of the ends it would have been shaped more like a V.

This, then, was what the men called a "frame." It was composed of fifteen timbers; and it measured thirty-six feet across, and twenty-four in depth. All these timbers have particular names. They are in two tiers, one laid over the other, on the platform, — "breaking joints," as the carpenters say; you know, — the ends of two sticks in one tier meet at about the middle of a stick in the other tier, to which they are bolted. First, across the bottom, is the "floor-timber"; then two "naval-timbers"; then a first, second, third, and fourth "futtock" (not "futtick" as the man said), in each arm of the frame; then a "stanchion" and a "top-timber" finish the arm. After the timbers were got into place, holes were bored, and long iron bolts driven through both tiers, four men driving one bolt, their four sledge-hammers revolving in the air and hitting the iron one after another, in complete time, making a lively scene.

When the frame was finished, pulley-ropes were made fast to it, and it was drawn off the platform down towards the ship, sliding flat along the keel, and a couple of planks were laid to support it, one on each side. When the bottom of the frame was near the standing frames, — the exact place for it being marked on the keel, — pulley-ropes were attached to the tops of the U, and it was raised right up into position, as neatly as anything you ever saw. The pulleys were worked by a capstan back in the yard. While this was getting into place, another frame was going together on the platform.

I climbed up into the half-finished skeleton, and looked around. On one side stood a twenty-foot ladder, with a man on the upper rounds, fastening the last frame to the others with a cleat. His head did not reach the top. The ship was still broader than she was deep; the bottom timbers forming an almost level floor for several yards each side of the keel. As I walked towards the stern she grew narrower, till finally the ribs crooked right up sharply from the keel, and there was no floor at all.

From the stern I looked out on the water, into which she was to be some day launched. The "ways" were already laid for her there, — timbers on blocks, like the two rails of a railroad, sloping down into the waves that were dashing over them.

The "stern-post" was not yet raised. It lay on a platform at the lower end of the keel, with the "transoms," or cross-timbers, already framed to it. This "post" is one of the strongest and most important timbers in the ship. It stands upright on the end of the keel, into which it is mortised. There is a groove cut in the back side of it, for the rudder-post to turn in. All the converging lines of the ship's under sides are brought into it with a graceful sweep. The transoms, and the stern-frame built out from them, make the broad and high part of the stern.

The frames in the bottom of the ship were set four inches apart. The two sets of timbers in each frame were bolted close together at the bottom; but up on the sides I noticed that pains had been taken to make an open space between them, — a wide crack. I asked a workman what that was for.

"Why, you see," said he, "a ship has to be preserved like so much corned beef or pork."

"How so?" said I.

"She has to be salted down," said he.

"Salted down!" said I, thinking he must be joking.

"To be sure," said he. "This 'ere ship's timbers would last a hundred years and more, if 't wa'n't for the dry rot. That's the ruination of vessels. It ain't like common rot; that goes to work in an honest kind of a way on the outside. Dry rot is sly; it begins its mischief on the inside of a timber, and turns it all to a kind of dry, crumbly powder, before ever you suspect it's there. I've seen a stick completely eaten up by it, while the painted outside remained as slick and han'some as ever."

I asked what occasioned the rot.

"That's more 'n I know," says he. "Some say it's a vegetable growth, — a sort of *fungus*, I believe they call it. The seeds are supposed to be in the sap of the tree, though I don't believe that, for timber that's been preserved hundreds of years will be attacked finally by the rot in certain situations. The planks we bend on to the bows and after-parts of the ship's sides have to be steamed; and it's found the dry rot don't attack them. These bottom timbers are protected by salt water, — that kills the rot, — but the upper timbers don't get the benefit of that, and so we salt 'em down. Them openings between 'em are all filled in with salt, when the frames are covered. It will take a hundred and eighty hogsheads of salt to salt down this 'ere ship."

That astonished me. Just think of it; a ship carries a small cargo of salt in the crevices between her ribs! The man hewed away a spell with his adz (he was smoothing the insides of the frames for the planks to be put on; he called the work "dubbing"), then looked up again and said, —

"The kind of cargo a ship carries makes all the difference in the world with the rot. She is lucky if she gets a cargo of salt for her first voyage. Spice — you would hardly believe it — is about the worst thing. I've known a new ship put into the spice trade to rot out in three years."

I looked over into a neighboring ship-yard, and saw the skeleton of a vessel nearly complete. So I thought I would go and see what was the next thing to be done. They were putting the keelson into her, — *kelson* the men call it, — a *son* of the *keel*, I suppose. It is a set of timbers inside the frames, running the length of the ship, corresponding with the keel outside. There were three courses of timbers, sixteen inches square, laid one on another, and making a pile ($16 \times 3 = 48$ inches) four feet high. These rested on the floor-timbers, which were eighteen inches thick. The keel under them was two feet. On the bottom of the keel was a five-inch plank "shoe." This made a "backbone" to the ship almost eight feet through! I must n't forget the "sister keelsons," — two strong timbers laid one on each side of the true keelson. Is n't there a backbone for you!

I asked the carpenter who gave me these figures

what the "shoe" was for. "It is a protection to the keel," he said. "If a ship strikes a rock, the shoe takes the brunt of the stroke, and often she may be got off by the shoe parting from the keel, and letting her slide."

They were putting on the top timbers of the keelson, and fastening them with bolts driven clear through into the keel. Such bolts! They were not driven by sledge-hammers, but by a sort of pile-driver, worked

BOLTING THE KEELSON.

by four men, who drew up the heavy iron weight by a pulley, and let it fall on the end of the bolt, which a fifth man guided.

In the yard some men were hewing out a rudder-post, — an immense timber thirty-six feet long. All the upper end of it was round as a mast; that comes up through a hole in the stern, and has the tiller attached to it. In large vessels there are ropes made fast to the tiller, and then to the wheel, so that the man at the wheel steers the ship. The rudder-post fits into the groove in the stern-post, upon which it is hung by pintles, — bolts making a sort of hinge. Only one side of the lower part of the rudder-post was rounded; some men were getting ready a stick of timber to be fitted to the other side, the upper end of it to come up as high as the top of the water after the ship was launched and freighted. Just these two timbers make the rudder that guides the ship. One would hardly think that turning it a little to the right or left would change her course so quickly! I suppose I need n't tell *you* that she can't be steered unless she is in motion. Leave the rudder alone, as she sails, and it will follow straight after the keel. But turn it ever so little, and the force of the water striking on one side pushes it off the other way, and the stern off with it. Moving her stern a little one way causes the bow to swing off in the opposite direction, you know; and this I believe is all the mystery there is in steering a ship.

The skeleton of this vessel was all complete except

a few of her bow timbers. Each rib in this part is framed and raised separately. It runs up to an astonishing height above the keel, — the bow being the loftiest part. The stem-post was nearly ready to raise. This is to the bow or stem what the stern-post is to the stern. It is an immense timber as large as the keel, into which it is framed, — or rather it is several timbers pieced together to give length, with the curve that shapes the prow. Where it joins the keel it makes almost a right-angle.

This point is called a "fore-foot." Behind the stem-post, curving with it, and secured to it, is a broad timber, or series of timbers, called the "apron." This is fastened to the keel by a "knee" (there are lots of knees in a ship). So you see her bow has one thing that belongs to a quadruped, another that belongs to a biped, and a third that belongs to both. I may add that her prow is her "head." A curious thing a ship, is n't she, though?

For some distance back of the lower part of the stem-post she is made so sharp, for cutting her way through the water, that there is no room for framing; so the thin space between her sides is there filled in with what is called dead wood, — heavy timbers nicely fitted and shaped, to bring, as you may say, the wedge to an edge. The stern, below the water-line, is as sharp as the stem, and I believe a little sharper; and the thin part there is filled in with dead wood just the same.

III.

FINISHING.

In the next yard was a ship nearly finished, and I went to take a look at her. There were three stagings built all about her, and men on them at work; and they kept up a jolly hammering and clattering, I tell you! A dozen men were carrying a long plank up an inclined plane, to the middle staging. It was of hard pine, five inches thick, six or seven broad, and fifty feet long. Six men at each end, with their shoulders under it, had hard work to get it up.

"They are putting on her *skin*," a workman told me. The *skin* I found consisted of such planks as these. She was already half covered, from the keel upwards. The planks upon her sides are thicker than those below, and are called "wales." I thought the big one the men were carrying up must be the Prince of Wales.

After they got it up on the staging, they placed it on the top of the planking already fastened to the timbers. As the ship's side bulged, while the plank was nearly straight, it had to be brought to its place by means of ring-bolts in the timbers, levers, ropes, wedges, and sledge-hammers. For the short curves about the bow and stern the planks have to be steamed, and put on wet and hot, or they would split all to pieces in bending. The wales do not run in straight horizontal lines, parallel with the ship's water-line,

BUILDING THE SHIP.

but they sweep from end to end in sagging lines, highest above the water at the bow and lowest about midships. The line of a ship's deck makes a similar curve. This is called the "sheer."

As soon as a plank was in place, it was fastened by spikes driven at each end. Afterwards auger-holes were bored at intervals clear through plank, timber, and inside plank, or "ceiling" (for this ship was already lined); then long wooden oak pins, called "trunnels" (though you won't find *trunnel* in the dictionary; the word is spelled *treenail*), were driven through, and wedged at both ends without and within. Besides these fastenings, iron bolts were let through and clinched on the inside.

The "skin" planks were cut so as to fit closely together against the timbers, and yet leave an open seam between them, a quarter of an inch wide, at the surface. On the lower staging the calkers were at work. Two men had eight or ten light iron wedges, which they drove into a seam, and opened it a quarter of an inch further. Other men followed, driving oakum in between the planks, with mallets and calking-irons. As fast as the head calker came up to the wedges they were knocked out, and oakum filled their place, while they were carried forward and driven into the seam again farther along. The ring of so many mallets made merry music, for a person who likes a lively noise. The oakum was driven in out of sight; it was afterwards to be covered with hot pitch from a syringe-like instrument, run along

THE CALKERS AT WORK.

the seam. This had been done in some places; and there carpenters were smoothing the planks all over with planes, and making the bottom ready for sheathing.

I went up to the top staging and climbed over on the upper deck, which men were calking in about the same way. Every exposed seam about a ship must be calked, you know, or the constant straining she gets in the heavy seas will make her leak like a sieve.

Carpenters were building the deck-houses and dressing the stanchion timbers, — the uppermost timbers of her frames, that rise above the deck and support her rails. The top rail is sometimes called a "monkey-rail." The wood-work between that and the water-ways is her "bulwarks." The "water-ways" are deep planks that form a way for the water about her deck (which is rounded a little, like a duck's back, so as to shed it), and let it out through holes called "scuppers." Secured to the stanchions, below the monkey-rail, is commonly another rail full of holes for wooden pins, to which the sail-ropes are made fast. This is the "pin-rail." The rail about the stern is the "taff-rail." You see every part of a ship has its peculiar name. I am going to get, if I can, some drawings, showing the principal parts, and send them to you.

From the upper deck (sometimes called the "spar-deck") I went down a steep ladder, through a "hatch-way" (sailors usually say simply the "hatch," as the "after hatch," the "main hatch"), and landed on the lower, or "main deck." There I had a good chance to see how she was finished up inside. Overhead, supporting the upper deck, and binding the two sides of the ship together, were "beams," extending across, and secured at each end by a naturally crooked piece of timber called a "knee." One end of this knee was fastened to the beam, the other to the side of the ship. There was another set of beams supporting

Midship Section (one side).

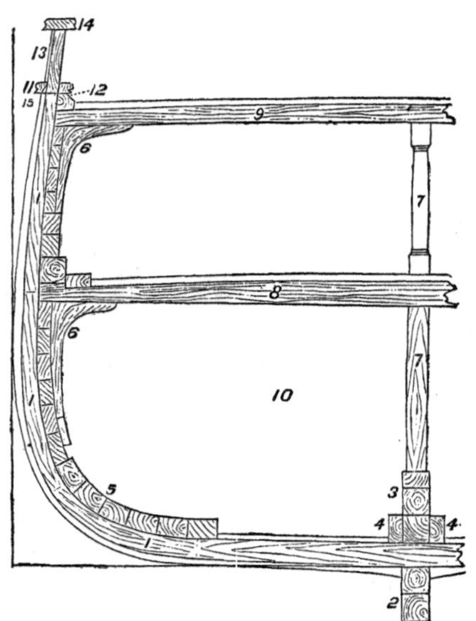

1, 1, 1. Timbers of the Frame	2. Keel.
3. Keelson.	4, 4. Sister Keelsons.
5. Ceiling.	6, 6. Knees.
7, 7. Hold and Between-Deck Stanchions.	
8. Lower, or Main Deck.	12. Water-Way.
9. Upper, or Spar Deck.	13. Bulwarks.
10. Hold.	14. Rail.
11. Plank Sheer.	15. Gunwale.

the deck under my feet. Besides the knees at the ends, each beam of the lower deck was supported at its centre by a stanchion, or prop, resting on the keelson. The beams of the upper deck had a row of just such stanchions, resting on the row below.

Through openings in the lower deck I could look down into the immense "hold." There were holes through both decks for the masts, which were to rest on the keel, secured to it by blocks called "steps." The "ceiling" — that is to say, the inside planking — was quite thin on the bottom of the hold. But it was made very heavy — a foot thick, I believe — where the sides began to rise, diminishing gradually to some seven inches between decks.

The clatter kept up inside that ship was jolly! The men were pounding down the ends of the bolts driven through from the outside; and then every stroke of the hammer or a calker's mallet on the "skin," or the deck above, was heard as plainly as if all these thirty or forty men were thundering away inside of her.

Some men were polishing down the beams and ceiling, and making them as handsome as the wood-work of the finest houses.

As I went out, and down over the side again, I saw a fellow bringing up coarse salt in a coal-hod and pouring it into the spaces between the timbers, which he kept filled as fast as the "skin" was put on.

The more I learned about a ship, and saw how skilfully designed and nicely fitted everything had to be, to give her symmetry and strength, and make her sit well on the water, the more I wondered at it; and it seemed to me one of the greatest mechanical feats to make the plan and patterns of a ship. I said as much to one of the carpenters, who replied, "You ought to visit a moulding-loft."

I asked what that was.

"The ship architect's workshop," said he, "where his model and the mould-boards are made. It 's a curiosity."

I asked, would the architect like to have me look in, — for of course I regarded him as a great man.

"Certainly," said he; "he 'll be glad to show you; and you 'll find him a perfect gentleman."

The carpenter gave me his address; it was only a few squares off. But, dear me, Mr. Clarence! I thought I could tell you all I had to tell on one sheet of paper, and at one sitting; now this is the third evening I have been writing, and I have n't begun to tell you the most interesting things about ship-building. So I 'll hold up for the present, and give you the rest in another letter.

Yours, out of breath,

LAWRENCE.

P. S. — I collected that bill!

IV.

THE MOULDING-LOFT.

A FEW evenings later Lawrence wrote: —

I began to tell you how I went to find the ship-wright, or ship architect, as they call him. I soon saw his sign on the upper story of a great, long old wooden building, near the ferry. At the top of two flights of stairs outside I came to a door with his name and slate on it; it was partly open, and I looked in.

It was a great room in the top of the building, at least a hundred and fifty feet long and thirty broad. On the sleepers overhead, beneath the roof, were piled all sorts of odds and ends of lumber. One side of the floor was occupied by piles of boards, carpenters' horses, benches, and tools; but the larger part was an open space, in the middle of which a man was at work on his knees, marking out lines by thin strips of boards or battens bent into curves, and held in place by awls stuck into the floor. He wore, tied on his knees, strong caps of leather, to protect them as he knelt at his work. I noticed that the toes of his shoes were worn through. He looked up pleasantly, under his broad-brimmed straw hat, and said, "Come in."

I told him frankly what had brought me there.

"That 's right; glad to see you," said he. "I 'll be through here in a few minutes, then I 'll show you."

I watched him at his work; and, looking around, saw that almost the entire floor was covered with long, sweeping, curved lines, in different groups, and straight lines running across them in places.

"Do you see what I am making here?" said he.

I said I supposed it must be the designs of a ship's timbers.

"You are right," said he. "These lines I am drawing now are for one of the ship's ribs. That is built up of several timbers; and I mark here a pattern of each. I cut out a mould-board after the pattern, and send that to the carpenter to cut his timber by."

"But how do you get your plan in the first place? That is what puzzles me!" I said.

He said he would show me that by and by, and kept on marking and talking. It was fun to see him bend a batten to just the curve he wanted, stick awls to hold it, and then mark his lines by it. He said it required five hundred moulds to make the timbers of a ship of the size he was designing (about thirteen hundred tons' burden); and it would take more than twice the number, "but," said he, "I make moulds for the timbers of only one side; and then there are several frames near the middle of the ship made just alike, from the same set of moulds."

I said, "I had no idea till to-day how much timber it took to build a ship!"

"It takes more," said he, "than can be got into another ship of the same size."

"What is the weight of such a ship as this when finished?" I asked.

"A thirteen-hundred-ton ship will weigh about nine hundred tons; that is, a wooden ship. An iron ship of the same capacity — "

"Will weigh considerably more, I suppose," I said, as he stopped to make some figures.

"Considerably less," said he. "An iron ship of thirteen hundred tons will weigh less than seven hundred tons."

"Do they build ships all of iron?" I asked.

"Yes; and they are the cheapest and best ships that can be made. The first cost is a third more than that of wooden ships; but they are more buoyant, they carry a larger freight, they are stronger, and they last three times as long. The dry-rot don't trouble them, and the water-worms let them alone. In place of these large timbers they have slender iron ribs; and in place of the heavy planking without and within they have just a thin skin of iron plates riveted together, less than an inch thick, except in very large ships. A great many ships are made of iron nowadays, especially in England, where iron is comparatively cheap and timber dear. The largest ship ever built is made of iron; that is the Great Eastern, — six hundred and eighty feet long by eighty-two and a half broad, and fifty-eight deep; a magnificent structure, though practically she don't seem to be good for much except laying Atlantic cables."

"What keeps an iron ship from sinking?" I asked. "The question came up at school the other day, and though we all seemed to know, yet not one of us, not even the teacher, could give a satisfactory answer. Iron will sink; then why don't an iron boat sink?"

"It seems to me you ought to answer that question," said he. "Why does wood float while iron does not?"

"Because," I said, "wood weighs less than the same bulk of water, while iron weighs more; and the heaviest substance goes to the bottom."

"In other words," said he, "wood, in order to sink, must displace more than its own weight of water. Now a boat is constructed in such a way as to displace a great deal more than her own weight of water by being made hollow. All the air she contains below her water-line is in the balance against an equal bulk of water outside. An iron ship, in fact, displaces just as much water as if she was built of solid metal. Let the water into her, and it drives the air out; then she displaces only the actual bulk of the iron, and down she goes.

"This question of displacement," he went on to say, "is a very important one in building a ship. We must know just how much water she will displace, in order to know what weight she will bear up. Now, thirty-five cubic feet of salt water weigh a ton. Salt water is heavier, you know, than fresh water; it takes thirty-six cubic feet of fresh water to weigh the same. A ton in our calculations is twenty-two hundred and forty pounds. Then for every ton's weight she buoys up she must displace thirty-five cubic feet of water. Her solid contents below her water-line will of course just equal the amount of water she displaces, — or, as we say in one word, the *displacement*."

I asked if it was by such calculations that a ship's tonnage was ascertained.

"When we speak of a ship of so many tons' burden, we mean the government rate. The government measures and rates every American ship. By the new rule the interior of a ship is measured, — just as you would get the solid contents of an odd-shaped box, — and every hundred cubic feet below her upper deck count for a ton. Some vessels will actually carry a good deal more than they are rated by this rule. Some kinds of freight — such as iron, and other solid matters — go by weight. Others — such as boxes of shoes — go by measurement, a certain bulk being considered equal to a ton."

"Do builders often make two ships from the same set of moulds?"

"Sometimes; but usually they prefer to have a new model for a new ship; perhaps they want to make her a little larger, or a little smaller, or sharper, or broader, or think they can improve upon the old model some way. Now step here, and I 'll show you what a model is. This is the first stage of it."

As I saw nothing but a bundle of plain boards in a press, I thought at first that he meant something else. There were, perhaps, a dozen boards, two thirds of an inch thick and about six feet long.

"After these are pressed firmly into shape," said he, "they are held together by screws, making what we call a block. Then we commence working it down to something like this shape."

He took me into a little workroom at the end of the loft, where a perfect little model — or, strictly speaking, half-model — of a ship lay on a work-bench. Imagine a ship sawed in two vertically in the centre from stem to stern, and one half of her will give you an idea of the form of this model.* Only it was

* Our model, deck plans, half-breadth and body plans, are from photographs of a model and drawings kindly furnished by Lawrence's friend, Mr. William H. Varney, Assistant Naval Constructor at the United States Navy-Yard, Portsmouth, N. H.

solid. Examining it, I found that it was carved out of just such a bundle of boards as I had seen; and the seams between them made so many parallel stripes, or water-lines, along the sides; only a top board had been added, thicker than the others, and carved so as to make the curved line, or sheer, higher at the bow and stern than amidships.

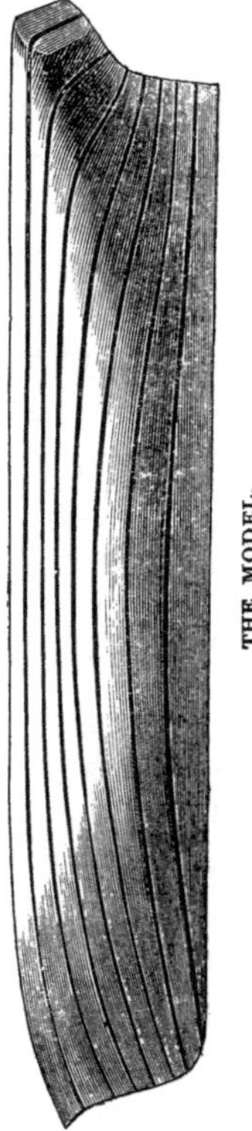
THE MODEL.

I asked why he did not carve his model from one solid block, instead of packing a pile of boards together.

"I 'll show you soon," said he. "This model is n't quite finished yet. I work it down till I think I have got it about right, or till the owner of the ship to be built from it is satisfied. When he comes in to see it to-morrow, he may say, 'Make her a little sharper,' — for the fancy is for sharp ships just now. There is this great advantage in making a model, — anybody can tell, by looking at it, just what the shape of the ship is to be. English shipwrights do not make models, but draw all their lines on paper first.

"The way we get our lines is this: When the model is completed I lay it on a smooth surface, flat side down, and mark around it, — that is, draw its profile. Then the water-lines are marked in. This forms what we call the *sheer plan.*

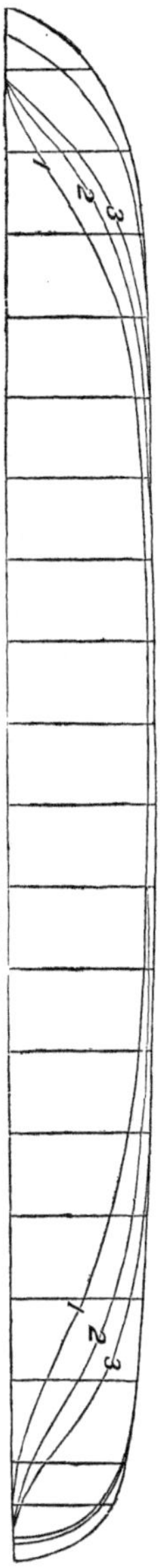

"Then I remove the screws, take the model to pieces, and lay one board after another, beginning with the narrowest at the bottom, on another plain surface, — the straight side of each being adjusted to a common centre-line, representing the centre of the ship. A line marked about the curved side of each board shows her exact proportions through that part which it represents. In this way we get what is called *the half-breadth plan.*

"By a scale of measurements we obtain from these two plans the exact dimensions of every part of the ship, and make a third plan, called the *body plan.* This represents her entire breadth and height, as viewed from one end, with curved lines on one side of a centre line showing the frame timbers of the forward half of the ship, and on the other side showing those of the after part.

"Now I 'll explain to you how we get out the designs of the frame timbers. The model is on a scale of one inch to three feet; that is, every inch

HALF-BREADTH PLAN. — 1, 2, 3, Water-lines.

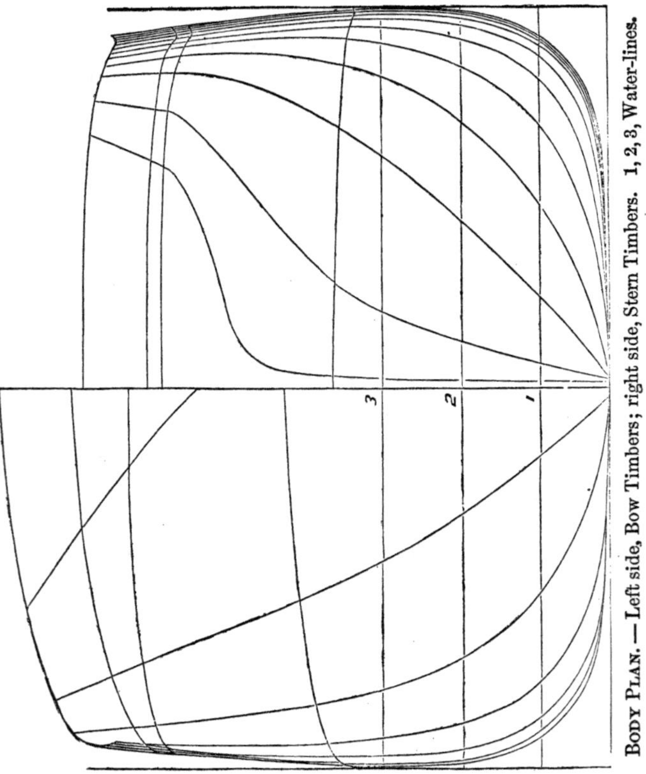

Body Plan. — Left side, Bow Timbers; right side, Stern Timbers. 1, 2, 3, Water-lines.

of the model stands for thirty-six inches in the ship to be built. Having got our body plan, therefore, we have only to draw it on the floor of the loft on a scale thirty-six times as large. Then every one of these curved lines represents a rib, for which we go to work and make as many moulds as are required."

"All that looks very simple now," I said. "But a man might learn it all by heart; still, it would bother him to build a ship!"

"I guess it would," said he. "For instance, a man comes to me and says, 'I want a steamboat for the cotton trade on a Southern river. She must carry three thousand bales where the water is only twelve feet deep.' I have to plan accordingly. Then one man wants a vessel for speed, while with another a heavy freight is the chief consideration. For speed, we make the model sharper, — on the principle that a knife will cut the water easier than a walking-stick will. But the sharper a ship, the less room she has for cargo. We make more room by building her broader but then she meets with more resistance passing through the water. Owners choose certain qualities for a ship, according to the trade she is in, — whether it is important she should go quickly with a light load, or leisurely with a heavy load. But it is n't all in her shape; she must be rigged right and loaded right to sail well."

I asked him if great improvements had not been made in modelling and rigging ships within a few years.

"We think so," he replied, with a smile. "A modern-built ship, designed for speed, — what we call a clipper ship, — will sail three times as fast as a ship built forty years ago; and it takes fewer men to manage her sails."

"What are the best proportions for vessels?" I asked.

"As a general rule the length of a ship is five times her breadth; her depth, one half or two thirds her breadth. Steamers are longer; a length equal to eight times the breadth is common. Length adds speed, but it weakens a vessel."

"When you get your floor covered with marks what do you do, — rub them out?"

"No; plane them off with what is called a lazy man's plane." And he showed me one; it had a handle like a mop, so that a man could use it standing.

V.

SPARS AND RIGGING.

In another room was his office; and there I saw several beautifully finished models of ships and steamers fastened to the wall, the pieces composing each having been finally glued together and polished up. I noticed that neither of them had the keel attached.

"No," he said; "the keel is n't necessary in a model, though it is indispensable in a ship. It not only gives strength, but a sailing vessel can't beat without it."

I told him I never could understand how a ship sailed *against* the wind.

"She can't sail directly against it," he said. "But she goes this way," — he drew a perpendicular arrow. "That represents which way the wind blows. Now suppose the ship's course lies in an opposite direction. But the nearest she can come to that is a line crossing the course of the wind something like this smaller arrow. Her sails are set diagonally, — this fashion, — so that the wind fills them, and presses them forward in the direction of this dotted line.

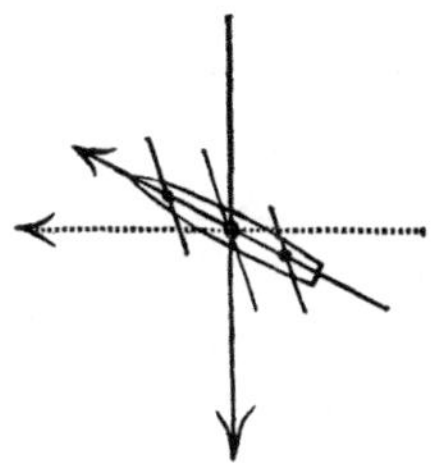

But a ship meets with great resistance going sidewise through the water; the keel is like a blade on the bottom; it adds greatly to that resistance, and serves to keep her in a straight course. So instead of sailing in the direction of the dotted line, she sails in the direction her keel points. But head her too much that way, and she drifts off with the wind. Some vessels will sail much closer to the wind than others. After she has sailed as long as the master thinks best in that direction her head is turned suddenly toward the wind; her momentum through the water keeps her in motion till she comes clear around, and gets the wind on her other side, and sails off on what is called another *tack.* In this way she describes a zigzag course against the course of the wind, sailing

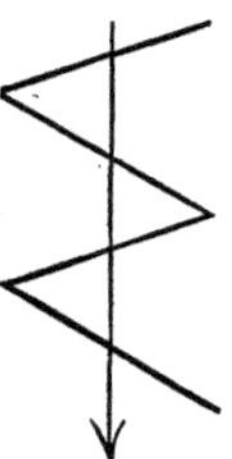

several miles for every one she makes in the direction she wishes to go. That is what we call *beating.* Some badly built or imperfectly rigged ships won't stay, — that is, they won't go around with their heads to the wind, but lose their momentum, and blow off; such ships, in tacking, have to *wear,* — turning the opposite way, with their sterns to the wind; a great disadvantage, as they necessarily go back a little on their course before they can get around on the other tack."

He took up a piece of wood from his desk, and, handing it to me, asked what I thought of it. I found it light as cork, and full of holes as a piece of honeycomb. It was a bit of ship's timber that had been destroyed by water-worms. The outer surface was smooth, appearing to be perforated here and there with pin-points. The worms were no larger than that, he said, when they went in; but, feeding on the wood, they grew rapidly, until they made a hole as large as a pipe-stem. They are *borers;* and, what is curious, the cutting end of a modern ship-auger is copied after their boring apparatus, and it is found to work better, in making a straight, deep hole, than any other.

"This ship," he said, "was loaded so that the water came above her sheathing; and so the worms got at her. A ship's bottom must be sheathed in some sort of metallic covering, or she is soon destroyed by insects, shell-fish, and marine vegetables, adhering to her. Copper makes the best sheathing, as it corrodes and poisons whatever touches it. But it is expensive, and it wastes rapidly; so a composition of copper and zinc is commonly substituted for it."

"When is the sheathing put on?"

"Sometimes just before she is launched," said he; "but it is liable to get injured when she goes off; and, besides, any leaks in her can't be so well detected and stopped afterwards. So she is usually launched first, and then taken to a dry-dock and sheathed. She is shut into the dock, the water is pumped out by steam-engines, and let in again after the sheathing is put on."

He told me ever so much about the spars and rigging, which I don't think I could write out if I should try. A *ship* is a vessel with three masts and square sails. A brig has two masts and square sails. A schooner has two masts with fore-and-aft sails. An hermaphrodite brig has the foremast square-rigged and the mainmast fore-and-aft rigged; she is half brig and half schooner. A sloop has only one mast. Then there is the topsail schooner, with a square topsail; and the barkantine, with three masts, the foremast rigged like a ship's, and the other two schooner-rigged.

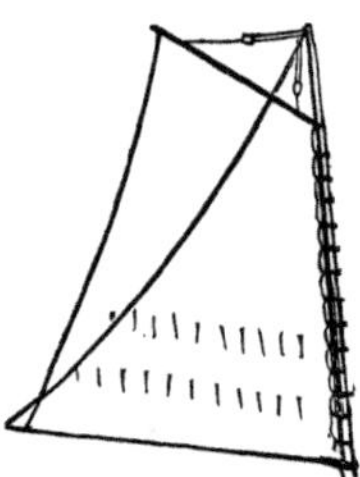

Fore-and-aft Sail.

The mast of a small vessel is generally a single well-rounded, tapering stick of pine. But each of the three masts of one of the largest ships consists of a number of sticks. The lower part of each has a central stick, and others fitted about it, — all well-rounded and hooped, to give greater size and strength. At the head of the lower mast is a platform called the "top." Standing on this is another mast, called the "topmast," — secured by a "cap." Atop of the topmast is the "top-gallant" mast; and over that the "royal." Some ships have besides what is called a "skysail mast," top of all. Each of these masts has a square sail of the same name hung upon it by a yard. The masts are held in their places by immensely large ropes, called "stays," and by smaller

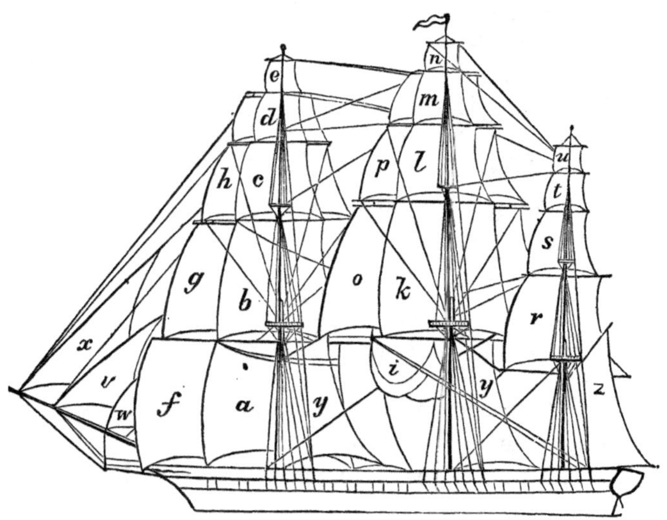

a. Foresail.
b. Fore Topsail.
c. Fore Top-gallantsail.
d. Fore Royal.
e. Fore Skysail.
f. Fore Studdingsail.
g. Fore Topmast Studdingsail.
h. Fore Top-gallant Studdingsail.
i. Mainsail.
k. Main Topsail.
l. Main Top-gallantsail.
m. Main Royal.
n. Main Skysail.
o Main Topmast Studdingsail.
p. Main Top-gallant Studdingsail.
r. Mizzen Topsail.
s. Mizzen Top-gallantsail
t. Mizzen Royal.
u. Mizzen Skysail.
v. Jib.
w. Fore Topmast Staysail.
x. Fore Staysail.
y. Fore and Main Spencers.
z. Driver or Spanker.

ropes called "shrouds," which also serve as ladders; the rounds, or steps, are cross-ropes, called "ratlines." The "halyards" are ropes for hoisting the yards and sails; the "braces" are for swinging them around; the "sheets" are ropes for hauling and fastening the lower corners of the sails. These, and other ropes used in managing the sails, are called the "running rigging." The stays, shrouds, etc., are the "standing rigging."

So much I remember. He has promised to get me a drawing of a full-rigged ship, and to mark in the names of the sails for me; if he does, you shall see it.

VI.

THE LAUNCH.

ALL at once, while I was talking with the shipwright, he looked at his watch.

"There 's to be a launch to-day at high tide," he said. "It 's almost high tide now."

You 'd better believe that excited me, for a launch was just what I wanted to see. I had passed right by the yard where it was to take place without knowing it. As I might have time to see it yet, if I hurried, I bade him good by, and went plunging down his outside stairs like a mad boy. Right under his loft was a rigging-loft, where men were at work making the stays and shrouds of ships, which I should have looked into, if I had had time; but the launch was the thing just then.

I arrived on the ground just in season. A crowd had gathered in the yard since I passed by; and another crowd was standing or sitting on the wharves or timbers of a neighboring yard, waiting to see the show. In ten minutes she would go off; and in the mean while I looked sharply about to see how the thing was to be done.

I told you of the ways laid on blocks, and extending down into the water from under the stern of the first ship I visited, — a sort of huge wooden railroad, you know. Well, a track like this had been built of timbers running from the water all along under the ship's bottom, on each side of her keel. It had a slope of nearly an inch to the foot, just enough to make her slide off handsomely.

She did not rest directly on these ways, understand. Built up all about her was a curious sort of frame, called a *cradle*, the bottom timbers of which are called *bilgeways*. These were the runners on which she was to take a ride down the track. She was blocked up by timbers and planks between her bottom and the bilgeways; and these rested on the ways, which had been well "greased with taller," as a workman informed me, and afterwards, when the tallow was cold, "slushed with ile and soft-soap." The under-sides of the bilgeways had also been greased. To prevent her from running off the track, strong hard-wood "ribbons" were fastened to the top of the ways on the outer edge, and well supported by slanting props set in the firm ground.

Her entire weight did not rest on the cradle as yet; otherwise there would have been nothing to prevent her from sliding down the slippery track. The piles of blocks on which she had been built were still under her keel, and a few shores at her sides. While I was looking on, the shores were taken away, and the word came to launch, when a number of men on each side, who stood ready with axes, commenced splitting out the top block of each pile.

I got a good position at a safe distance on a pile of lumber near the saw-mill. The crowd was perfectly silent, waiting to see the huge thing start; and there was scarcely any noise but the sound of the axes, and the puffing of the steam-tugs lying off the yard waiting to catch her as soon as she was launched.

"I hope the tugs will do better than they did with the last ship I saw go off," said a man who stood on the boards beside me. "She was a very large ship; the cables parted they undertook to hold her with; she got away, and ran clean across the stream, butted agin the navy-yard wall, poked her nose into it fifteen feet, and there stuck."

As he had broken the silence, I asked, "Do they always launch stern-foremost?"

"Oftener than any other way," he said. "Sometimes they launch bow foremost. Very large vessels in narrow streams have to be launched sideways. The Great Eastern was launched sideways in the Thames."

The men had begun splitting out the blocks nearest the water. I supposed they would have to split out the top block on the last pile under the bow before she would start. But half a dozen piles still remained untouched, when suddenly the crowds on each side shouted, "She is going!" The men with the axes sprang away, while the last blocks whirled over beneath her keel, as her weight came down on the bilgeways, and they began to slide. It was a grand sight, — that immense structure, a ship of the largest size, starting slowly at first, then moving off faster and faster, striking the water, and throwing up a great wave as she plunged in! You never heard heartier cheers! I cheered and swung my hat till everybody else was done, I was so excited. The tugs held her; and then we cheered again. Everybody likes to see a great enterprise carried out with such perfect success; and building and launching such a vessel is one of the grandest.

There were a few gentlemen and ladies aboard of her, when she went off; and how I envied them! Yet people said the sight was better from the shore.

Well, it was all over; and what astonished me as much as anything was the hole she made in that yard after she had gone off. Imagine a meeting-house in a village square suddenly disappearing, leaving it vacant, and a crowd of people around the spot where it stood, and you 'll have some idea of it.

This ship had been sheathed before she was launched. As the tugs began to move off with her down the stream, I asked where she was going.

"To the shears," said some one.

I asked what the "shears" were, and was told that they were a couple of spars lashed together, set upright, and furnished with tackle for lifting the masts into and out of vessels. I ought to have told you before, that a vessel's spars (which include masts, yards, bowsprit, boom, etc.) are not put in till after she is launched.

It was too late for me to visit the shears; and I guess you are glad of it,— for have n't I written you another stunningly long letter? The shears, instead of cutting it short, would only make it longer.

Good by.

LAWRENCE.

INDEX.

THE END.

Cambridge: Electrotyped and Printed by Welch, Bigelow, & Co.

www.ingramcontent.com/pod-product-compliance
Lightning Source LLC
LaVergne TN
LVHW010253110826
845151LV00004B/1464

* 9 7 8 1 4 2 5 5 2 2 7 7 3 *